Team Secrets
of the
NAVY SEALs

Team Secrets
of the
NAVY SEALs

The Elite Military Force's Leadership
Principles for Business

Robert Needham

Skyhorse Publishing

Skyhorse Publishing books may be purchased in bulk at special discounts for sales promotion, corporate gifts, fund-raising, or educational purposes. Special editions can also be created to specifications. For details, contact the Special Sales Department, Skyhorse Publishing, 307 West 36th Street, 11th Floor, New York, NY 10018 or info@skyhorsepublishing.com.

Skyhorse® and Skyhorse Publishing® are registered trademarks of Skyhorse Publishing, Inc.®, a Delaware corporation.

Visit our website at www.skyhorsepublishing.com.

10 9 8 7 6 5 4 3 2 1

Library of Congress Cataloging-in-Publication Data is available on file.

ISBN: 978-1-61608-342-7
2012 Barnes and Noble edition ISBN: 978-1-4351-4023-3

Printed in China

Contents

Introduction

Background of the Teams

Since the establishment of our force, Frogmen have willingly put themselves at risk so that others may live free and fruitful lives. The men of Naval Special Warfare (NAVSPECWAR) are willing to go places and do things others cannot or will not.

Naval Special Warfare has always been and always will be a strictly volunteer organization. If at any time a Frogman wishes to leave, he may do so. When a Team member is unwilling to complete an assigned task, there is no sense in bringing him along; others are already waiting for the opportunity to prove their mettle. This important parallel to the business world is the basis of the lessons in this book.

In World War II, U.S. forces took heavy losses because of their inexperience with amphibious operations and at acquiring intelligence. Procuring information about the composition of beachheads, the firmness of the sand, and the location of sandbars, coral reefs, and man-made obstacles became absolutely imperative. The technology behind today's satellites, which provide immediate and up-to-date imagery, was still decades away. The question was how to get such detailed and current information. The answer was Naval Combat Demolition Units (NCDUs), amphibious reconnaissance forces that operated in advance of conventional troops at great personal risk.

These Frogmen were men so dedicated to their country that they were willing to do whatever was asked of them. They often went into combat wearing only swim trunks, a knife, a mask, fins, and a satchel of explosives. This earned them several monikers; the two most noted and cherished being "naked warriors" and "Frogmen." In a time before wet suits, these men of iron resolve would cover their bodies with axle grease to fight off the bone-chilling waters of the Atlantic.

Over time, the forces became known as UDTs (Underwater Demolition Teams). During the Korean War, the UDTs began a transition to hinterland operations, conducting small demolition raids. After the Korean War, the need for anti-guerrilla warriors was recognized. In 1961, President Kennedy commissioned the first two SEAL Teams (Sea, Air, Land Teams) to conduct "unconventional warfare." (SEAL Team One was based on the West Coast, SEAL Team Two on the East Coast.) UDTs were still in existence; however, they were slowly phased out over the next few decades as more SEAL Teams were commissioned.

SEALs saw their first combat during the Vietnam War, earning them a reputation as the most ruthless operators, accepting and completing missions that others would not even consider. Although SEALs were killed, not one was ever left behind or captured. This is a fact that all SEALs value and live by, and it is the basis of the Team concept.

From the very first days of the Frogman lineage up to the time this book was originally published, only 240 classes and a handful more than 6,500 men have made the grade. To date, this number has risen into the 270s. These new Frogmen joined the most elite fighting force knowing that they would be thrust deep into the quagmire of today's chaotic and tumultuous combat environment. They take this obligation freely, not for the fame, or the glory, or even the proverbial t-shirt. They endure unimaginable hardships to combat our current and most determined enemies.

SEALs have monopolized the news in the past few years, much to their chagrin, because SEALs are private warriors. SEALs are executing the most difficult, demanding, and seemingly impossible missions. The ability to achieve at this level is born from basic leadership and team dynamic fundamentals. I have been fortunate to serve among such men. I have learned equally from subordinates and superiors alike, and learned that rank does not guarantee the greatest insight. I have had the unprecedented opportunity to interact and build friendships with true heroes from the beginning of the Frogman history at our yearly reunions. They are not just for a specific Team, but for ALL Frogmen, from the dawn of Naval Special Warfare. Although they are the most ruthless of warriors, you will find that most SEALs are devout family men full of warmth and the desire to succeed in any situation and assist anyone who truly believes in the same principles. I owe the Naval Special Warfare community a debt of gratitude that could not be repaid in forty lifetimes. I remain active in fund raisers to support NAVSPECWAR and the families of the operators. Although I am a member I still donate monies and time in this pursuit.

To date, not one man involved in a SEAL operation has ever been left behind. Every avenue is exhausted to bring them home dead or alive. It is the strength and core of a lifelong and indestructible fraternity. It's what makes a Team Guy a Team Guy. Long live the Brotherhood.

Leadership is risk, management is safe.

Chapter 1

~

Leading the Best

Navy SEAL Concepts for Leading Professionals and Team Building

Every moment of a SEAL's life is geared toward the development, education, and honing of the Team! The word "Team" encompasses everything from the sixteen-man platoon to our entire country and way of life. In the Teams, men work relentlessly with their fellow Frogmen and face incredible odds to accomplish their assigned tasks, whether this is the daily routine of gear maintenance in preparation for future operations or the planning and execution of a real-world mission. Most SEAL's transition to the private sector carrying the same ethos and unflappable attitude and demeanor, and apply it to their civilian lives. Many of my former Teammates are now top executives or successful business owners, applying what they learned and nurtured in the SEAL Teams to achieve positive results.

What would you think if your boss told you that you were going to push a boat out of an airplane at night and then jump out after it, deploying your own parachute and chasing the boat to the water with seven other people and without the aid of an overtly visible light source? As the bite of the cold night air, the rush of the wind tearing at your gear and stark darkness attempt to dull your senses, your honed skills and adrenaline "defog" your consciousness. The possibility of entangling your parachute with another jumper is extremely high in the violent and rapid evolution. The jump is too low to even bother bringing a reserve. Without words the seasoned Team finds their way to the boat which just splashed down. One by one the jumpers splash into the cold ocean. Next, you'll need to maneuver out of your parachute as the sea current turns your once life-saving parachute into a deadly sea anchor, capable of drowning the strongest waterman, and get the boat operational in ten minutes, engines mounted and running, because you have to pick up eight more men who are about to jump into the cold, dark night and splash into the water. Then you'll have navigate the open ocean to a point at which you will then need to paddle for about an hour so as to not alert anyone to your presence with the hum of a motor. Get in, get it done, and get out, all under the cloak of one night's darkness. A sixteen-man Team, two officers and fourteen enlisted men, complete all the planning, preparation, coordination, supervision, and execution of such a mission ... and that's your Monday and Tuesday.

Every day of this week and the next, and the next after that, you will be responsible for the lives of your crew, either in training or in combat. The only way you can survive is to trust your Team and be trusted by them. You can't think only of yourself and those factors affecting or stressing your life. Everyone's life depends on each member thinking as one. The "poor me" attitude is poison and is a major hurdle in any group dynamic.

This is my life, and this is how I survive. The principles of SEAL leadership and cohesiveness apply to all groups; and strong Teams, in business and in life, are ruthlessly effective in achieving their common goals.

I am currently serving my nineteenth year of active duty and will not use the real names of any of my brothers, specific Operation names, nor specific locations and times. It is my desire to remain anonymous, but thanks to the Internet, that is nearly impossible. Many of my closest friends are also still on active duty, and it would be inappropriate to proffer their identities.. Those who have gotten out are all private men and appreciate their anonymity and were never in it for the glory…only the grave responsibility of our country's defense and to be part of the finest Team I have ever had the honor to be part of. I have built this book, however, with stories from my own experience. Lead by example, build a stronger Team, and, over time, you will create a successful business and career. This isn't a book of combat tactics or detailed war stories. It is a series of snapshots of the more than nineteen years of my military career and the trials and errors I have gone through during this chapter of my life. This is what I have found to be effective across a wide spectrum of challenging situations. This should be a quick read, and one I hope you revisit from time to time to refresh your memory and reacquaint yourself with the solid fundamentals of Team building and broadening. This will not be, nor should it be, the last book published on leadership. Continue to explore techniques and flex with the changes. There is room on the "lessons learned" pages to write your own. This book is the foundation for a working document on leadership.

Basic Philosophy of the Teams: Volunteer Program

To get a shot at SEAL training, you must exhibit initiative and determination. It isn't easy to get into BUD/S (Basic Underwater Demolition/ SEAL), which is the initial training program SEALs must go through. Determination is the key. Out of about every 300 men who say they want to be SEALs, probably 100 mean it, and only about twenty actually make the necessary effort. The day I tested, only five of seventeen sailors passed the initial screening for BUD/S. And even then, inclusion was not guaranteed. It took me over eight months to convince my command to let me go and secure orders to BUD/S.

Over a year after my initial screening I arrived in sunny Coronado, California, to attend BUD/S at the Naval Special Warfare Center. My class started with 129 men who swore they wouldn't quit. After seven months, 114 couldn't keep their word or were seriously injured.

The daily BUD/S schedule was part of the reason. In the First Phase, the initial aspects of Team building weed out those who do not desire to put forth the effort required to continue with training. The days and nights are filled with a series of physical and mental challenges, called evolutions, performed in a continuous rotation. Each shift brings fresh instructors, every one ready to dole out the next set of obstacles. During the rite of passage referred to as "Hell Week," usually the fifth or sixth week of training, a man will get no more than an hour and a half of sleep, total, from Sunday morning to Friday evening, all the while moving and thinking, nonstop. This is the "application process," and it reveals who really wants to be here and, more importantly, who possesses the required raw talent and intellect.

In the Second Phase, the physical standards get tougher, and an intense diving curriculum begins. The underwater aspect of SEAL operations is extremely serious, and those who don't have the physical stamina, or can't keep their wits about them underwater in the pitch dark, tend to volunteer to leave the program here. The academics get harder. This is the "first interview" phase. You want to be here, you have what it takes to be here, now…we have a few questions for you.

The Third Phase demands that sailors reach the highest physical and mental standards. This is also the phase where they up the stakes by introducing live fire ranges, dynamic and static, as well as live land and underwater demolition, the root of our existence. However, not many men are lost during this phase, because those who would prefer another profession and those who could not meet the strength and academic requirements have already quit.

Throughout this training, SEAL instructors never let you forget that you are seeking membership in a volunteer organization. They realize that they may someday work with you and that their lives will depend on your competence. They have a vested interest in the quality of their students. In the meantime, they continually monitor those who are wavering and offer to help these men find a different niche in the Navy if it turns out that being a SEAL is not their priority.

Team Concepts for the Individual:*Never Quit!*

If you have been assigned a task, you had better seriously evaluate your ability to complete it beofre accepting it. There is no honor in undertaking a remarkably daunting task if you can't get it done *correctly*. This is not to say that you should shelter yourself in menial tasks to avoid the possibility of failure, but should carefully assess the situations at hand and take on any challenge you feel that, through the combined effort of you and your Team, you will be able to accomplish. Moreover, remember that once you have committed, you are in. If you suddenly find that you're in over your head, you had better sprout gills and come up with a way to complete the task properly. If you need to reset, do so after careful consideration of the consequences and after developing other possible solutions. Simply throwing your hands in the air ... like you, well, just don't care is admitting defeat and quitting.

The reasoning behind the intensity of any training program is, and should be, to identify those who are going to be there; ready to succeed when it counts. Job titles may sound glamorous, but you need to know who is going to be there when the Team needs them the most. Who in your group is the most qualified or best able to tackle a problem? If the person that usually collates your meeting handouts has a talent useful in solving a task someone else is struggling with, bring them into the fold and grow as a unit. You may be amazed at what you find waiting in the minds of those you might usually overlook.

You Are Only as Strong as Your Weakest Team Member

"Weakest" may simply refer to the Team member carrying the heaviest load. This can be directed or self-incurred. In a SEAL platoon, the communications man usually carries the most weight. Every man in the SEAL Platoon is ready to fight as any other. However, certain members carry an extra burden due to their specialty. The communicator is required to carry his radios, antennas, and extra batteries, all this in addition to the standard war fighting load required to be carried by all. The machine gunner must carry his heavy weapon and the mass amount of ammo required to feed his machine. These men are not weak, but will most likely be the slowest and most encumbered members. It goes without saying that each member will carry an extra battery and an extra 100-200 rounds of ammunition for the machine gunner. If the point man (usually the person with the lightest load) leading the platoon maintains a rapid pace, he will likely exhaust and unnecessarily wear out these crucial members of the unit.

A Team leader must have a reason for picking and tasking each member of the Team. Recognize, utilize, and capitalize on the attributes on which you based your choices. Make these choices and reasons apparent to the group so all know what the focus and intent is.

Surround yourself with "operators," those who perform, always being mindful of the difference between the person you just like to have around and the one you and your Team need to succeed. Job assignment is not a popularity contest; you should always choose the best person for each job. Personality is crucial in many positions; especially those positions that require interactions with others. Or maybe you need a person that 'lacks' some personality to handle situations that must remain devoid of emotion. All this said, pick by merit and application rather than popularity.

An important thing to remember: just because someone is new, that doesn't mean they will not be able to improve upon the way business is conducted. I have noticed that at times "old guys" will ignore the "new guys" simply because they are new.*Never*underestimate the value of a fresh, innovative, and perhaps even abstract point of view. Diversity is good and can strengthen the Team.

SEAL Training and Common Goals

SEAL instructors challenge themselves and each other to develop "innovative" techniques to embed the necessity for solid and cohesive teamwork from day one of training. Everything is done as a class, which is identified by that unique and sequential set of seemingly insignificant numerals. This number becomes your life, your burden, your salvation. A Frogman NEVER forgets his class number. It validates you with other SEALs and immediately identifies your spot in Naval Special Warfare history as the time stamp for your indoctrination into the brotherhood. The men eat as a class, move as a class, physically train as a class, learn as a class, suffer as a class, fail as a class, succeed as a class, celebrate as a class, and graduate as a class. If one man screws up (the weak link for that evolution), everyone joins him in performing the assigned penalty, thereby motivating the entire class to attend to the weak member's deficiencies. You fail as a Team and succeed as a Team. However, there are times when it is appropriate and necessary to address the individual or a small portion of your greater group as such. At times, if there is a noticeable disparity between particular segments of the class, instructors will give the least performing portion a bit of "extra instruction" while those whom performed better are rewarded with a relatively easier tasking. This is healthy competition which is also Team building. Those who have achieved are the positive example and set the bar higher, urging the others to excel. You must be aware of the weaker links but work together to improve their performance in the long run, rather than continually holding your excelling performers back.

A BUD/S class is broken down into Boat Crews of six or seven men. The crews are periodically reorganized when people quit, but this will not happen until the instructor staff is ready to do so. So, as people fail, the remaining members of the Team are required to endure the increased burden until they can gain new members. After the reorganization they must learn quickly to work the newer members into the Team's cohesiveness and work through personality differences in order to succeed. As the name suggests, each Team has the charge of a boat. An IBS (inflatable boat, small) resembles a white-water raft. Two of the most memorable Team-building exercises executed as a boat crew were Log P.T. (physical training) and surf passage (with the IBS). Both of these tasks are capable of causing serious injuries and nearly impossible to perform without solid and cooperative actions.

Log P.T. is done as a Boat Crew with a fifteen-foot section of a telephone pole. The instructors run the men through a series of exercises with the log, each requiring the efforts of the entire Boat Crew. If one person slacks off, the others will be required to tackle the added burden until completion, or until motivating the slacker to get back in the game.

For example, in such exercises as Boat Crew sit-ups, each man cradles his section of log in his arms, and at the instructor's command will be required to perform a simple sit-up. If everyone shifts their weight and strains their muscles in unison, this task is doable, but is extremely grueling after an hour or so. Once any members begin to lose the will or mental toughness to continue, the seed of failure is sown. Another Team building exercise is to have the crew stand in a line, front to back; the instructor tells you which shoulder they want the log on. The crew needs to work together to get it up, over their heads, and back to the proper shoulder. Easy, right? Once fatigue takes its grip, the simple can seem daunting. Say not everyone lifts at the same time, starting a ripple that shifts the weight rapidly and becomes hard to control. Releasing the weight too early can cause the log to come crashing down on a man's head. Often you find that you and your crew are holding the log at arm's length over your heads until the instructor gets tired. My personal favorite was the foot races in soft sand with the log on your shoulders. In order for the entire crew to "get on the log," they'd have to turn their bodies forty-five degrees to one side, which made it even harder to run. Feet and legs crash together as everyone attempts to match the other's gait. The crew is jammed on the log, and it takes maximum Team coordination to prevent feet from entangling and bringing the crew to the ground in a pile of limbs followed closely by the three-hundred-pound log. Your mind tells you that your arms and shoulders are depleted of strength, and many crews would fail this test repeatedly. Those who stick around continually experience these evolutions and learn that it is not the muscles that give out, but the mind. Crews could not leave until they completed this task. I can remember occasions when it took my crew a dozen attempts before success; we would wonder how we got it the twelfth time but couldn't do it the first time. That is what BUD/S and Team building is all about:persevering until success!

In surf passage, the Boat Crew is required to paddle the boat through the pounding surf zone to the relative calm of the waters beyond. One man calls the cadence while the rest paddle in unison to attain this common goal. This is a difficult evolution, especially during the winter months because the waves are huge and can easily flip the IBS end over end, mangling and twisting the boat and its crew. If just one man stops paddling or gets out of sync in that crucial moment while tackling a big wave, the entire crew will pay as the powerful wave tosses them about like rag dolls. One instructor used to tell us that the "dumper" is out there, that rogue wave waiting to spring on the unprepared and undisciplined. You are a Team, but someone must be in charge, even if only for that unique event. In the simple evolutions I just described, dissent among the members or the failure to work in unison to the leader's tasking will result in disruption, and possibly serious injury if the "dumper" shows up. To top it off, these are all races and a competition with the other crews.

It Pays to Be a Winner!

Nearly every evolution in BUD/S pits the Boat Crews against one another in healthy competition, commonly in the form of races, where the men run while carrying either the boat or the log as a crew, or paddle to designated points. The winning Boat Crew is often rewarded by the opportunity to sit out the next race or receive early release from that particular training evolution. BUD/S is geared towards teaching the class to operate as a unit, but in keeping with the weeding out, or "interview process," there must be competition and there must be reward for those who continue to produce results time and again. Team members can't help but form ties when they work closely together to achieve a common goal. Naval Special Warfare is unique in the Department of Defense in that officers and enlisted men endure the exact same training, mixed in the same class. All members of the SEAL Teams have the same basic training and skill sets, and though some men hold positions of leadership, many hold different ranks, and others have attended specialty schools to develop unique and crucial war fighting skills, they are first and foremost, members of the brotherhood, members of the Team. Once you graduate from BUD/S, the "pays to be a winner" mindset manifests itself in healthy completion during morning P.T., success on the objective, and the ability to come home.

Natural Selection

Through these evolutions, the class inevitably sheds some weight. As members of the Boat Crews drop out and crews are reassigned, new Teams form. It is imperative that the new crew members adapt, learn one another's strengths and weaknesses, and prepare to face the instructor's next labyrinth of trials. It's all business—the individual does not have the luxury of lamenting over his buddy who decided to quit. At every turn, each man is reminded that he is there only because he wants to be. A BUD/S student can, at any time, stop the pain and stress whenever he wants to simply by telling the instructors that he has had enough and wishes to quit by stating, "I, D. O. R." (drop on request). This particular school is designed to test every last ounce of resolve a prospective SEAL has, down to the base instincts of survival. The standard of success has been set and refined by Naval Special Warfare and it is strictly adhered to. To be successful you must decide what attributes, skill sets, and mental capacity you require of your Team members. Find them, recruit them, test them, and develop them. During this process you must stick to your standards to ensure the greatest opportunity for success.

Results

As a professional, you have a job to do. The previous examples of Team building may seem like excessively harsh training that results in staggering attrition, but such culling is necessary if you want to select only those who will not quit when it counts. The purpose of weeding out the unfit is strikingly evident when you proudly sit among those who've decided to stay and work for the Team. The internal and group pride experienced when, through hard work, personal sacrifice, and downright intestinal fortitude, the Team is triumphant, is infectious and emotionally fulfilling. Even in failure, a tight Team can learn, adapt, train, and get itself back in the fight.

If you make it through all the trials, you join a Team made up of life-long friends with a "sea bag" full of confidence, stories worth telling, an enhanced appreciation for the human spirit, and an unrivaled sense of what a true Team is.

Personal Accountability

Personal accountability is the next important lesson. If you have built a good Team, you are expected, as are the rest of the members, to be of the highest caliber. Hold yourself to these standards as you would anyone else ... no excuses. If you allow yourself to compromise this tenet, the members of your Team will come to realize that you are not doing your part as a leader and Team member. This is hard to recover from, so don't let it happen in the first place.

Real Work

A member of an operational SEAL platoon can figure that about sixty percent of the men around him are experienced SEALs. The rest are new members, affectionately known as "meats." Each platoon's objective is to complete a yearlong workup to prepare for a six-month deployment. And, just like a Teamgroup of professionals building through development in their particular specialty, a platoon will participate in several phases of training, to learn and then hone their skills and tactics in several areas. Each block, or phase, will follow the same basic pattern: Learn, apply, review, evaluate, reapply, reevaluate, and then set SOPs (standard operating procedures). Once set, SOPs can decrease the time required to complete repetitive tasks, avoiding the need to reinvent the wheel. These are solid building blocks from which to grow. If you find a better method, change the SOP!

Getting a job done fast is fruitless if it isn't done right. The quality of the end result is not only important for "customer" satisfaction; it is also paramount for the sense of accomplishment felt by your group. Individuals and Team crews must constantly evaluate their progress. If an individual or Team starts to lose focus, they must take a step back and review. When you are planning a mission or a roadmap to complete an assigned task, set points along the way to realign and refocus your efforts. Bring the Team together and ensure that you are indeed headed in the correct direction. You will most likely require your Team to split into smaller groups to accomplish tasks more efficiently and rapidly. These periodic check points will ensure you're on track. During a patrol or dive, we designate points along our route where we stop and check timing, location, and the most up to date intelligence to ensure we are headed for the correct target and that the expected conditions are still manageable and suitable for success. Arriving on the objective or showing up to a presentation only to find that the circumstances changed days ago can result in failure.

It is incumbent upon any group that desires true success to set an environment that allows and encourages communication. As a Team member, you can't be afraid to admit that you do not understand the goal or have a concept of the operations that will get you there. If the crew is only as fast as its slowest man, you cannot remain silent for fear of retribution, hoping that you will catch up. You must honestly evaluate your own ability and communicate forth-rightly about it—for your own good and for that of the Team. If everyone else is unaware of a weak link, they cannot repair it. Unnoticed, the weak link will break, costing money, time, and perhaps even lives.

One block of training for a SEAL platoon is land warfare, which consists of a wide array of combat tactics, most of which are conducted using live ammunition and live explosives. Particularly dangerous are IADs (immediate action drills), designed to teach a platoon tactics and methods of breaking contact with an enemy force. These involve shooting, moving, and communicating through various types of mental and environmental conditions in order to evade enemy fire.

In this loud and chaotic environment, the trainers keep the pressure on by setting off small explosives to keep the heat on, enhance the experience, and let the Teams know that the "enemy" is still out there. As the platoon sustains fire, the platoon OIC (officer in charge) looks for a way out. He must, in a matter of seconds, use his experience, training, and intuition to identify hazards and find a safe escape route. The price for slow or bad decision making is that the training cadre will start "killing" his men. Now the fighting force is reduced and much less effective, as not only is one gun offline due to the "injury," but one or two more are offline because they have to carry the wounded man out of the beaten zone.

In addition, each man needs to be aware of the condition of his firearm at all times. When a man gets his turn to jump up and run, he must flick on his safety and be careful not to sweep his buddies with his rifle muzzle, as a hot gun can "cook off" a round at any time. (A cook-off is when the chamber of the gun is hot enough to cause the round sitting in it to combust, inadvertently firing the weapon.) Since everyone is nearly deafened by the noise of gunfire and explosions, each man screams to pass the "word" (instructions) to the next man. This is not the time to play catch-up. When a man doesn't know what's going on, which way to go, or where his people are, he can end up shooting someone or getting shot himself. This is not the time to realize that you don't have an intricate understanding of your Team's SOPs.

In short, what's important to the SEAL Team is important to any team of professionals in business: Stay informed, stay alert, and stay alive.

Innovative Thinking

The unwillingness or inability to think creatively will not only hinder your group's progress, it will stifle the young and creative untapped innovators in your organization. The majority of people want to achieve, want to be heard, and want to be part of a successful unit.

Make an anonymous suggestion box available. Let people get rankling details, complaints, or serious concerns off their chests. These may be issues or conditions that they are afraid of, embarrassed by, or unsure of, which bog them down. Provide a release valve. As a leader, invite Team members to identify themselves when they drop off suggestions, pointing out that if they do, you can get in touch with them for further discussion but don't make it a requirement.

You may find that most messages are nothing but empty complaints. It is imperative that you stress that no issue will be addressed unless the author also includes a viable solution, which will show that they truly seek improvement rather than empty belly aching. This will foster an atmosphere of ownership, as well as innovative and fresh thinking among Team members.

If someone comes to you with a new idea, at the very least consider it. Barking, "We've done it this way for years and it works fine!" will do nothing but stifle those around you. No one will want to bring that next "million dollar" idea to you if they perceive through your previous actions that their ideas will be crushed and discounted.

Challenge your Team to think outside the box, brainstorm, and create. Give them the responsibility and the latitude to be creative.

Be Serious, but Don't Take Yourself So Seriously

Finding the bright side of a bad situation is better than losing your motivation. I recall one of my first big training missions as a newly designated SEAL, huddled in a tiny hide, dug into the earth and surrounded by vegetation, nearly motionless to avoid detection while enduring miserable conditions. Shaking from the cold and soaking wet from three days of rain, the air temperature vacillating between thirty-four and thirty-eight degrees Fahrenheit, I turned to my platoon mate and whispered, "Damn, this sucks." He replied with a toothy grin, "Yeah, but it will make a great story later." We did our best to stifle and muffle our low chuckles. Then he reached into his rain jacket and handed me a piece of cherry licorice. There is warmth and shelter in camaraderie built in the pursuit of a common goal. If you can find humor in a bad situation and joke about it, you will have a better chance of salvaging your attitude and coming out on top.

CHAPTER 1 LESSONS

- You succeed as a team or fail as a team.
- To develop Team skills and to operate accordingly takes time and concerted effort.
- Improve the quality of your Team by truly screening your prospective Teammates. Thorough screening sets the standard from day one.
- Accountability is paramount and necessary.
- Periodically evaluate progress as a group to ensure everyone is still headed to the same rendezvous point or objective.
- Encourage Team members to bring forth their ideas and complaints.
- Challenge your group to keep their brains turned on and active.
- Enjoy the ride, thrive on the challenges, and appreciate your accomplishments.
- Some of the most daunting periods can be the makings of the greatest stories and memories.

Chapter 2

Know
Who You've Got

You Must Know Your Team and What Motivates Them

Merely directing day-to-day routine operations and thinking of those under you as nameless workers is simply "managing." This was well and good forty years ago, when companies demanded marginally educated employees willing to perform the same tasks for eight to ten hours a day. But it is terribly wasteful in an era when higher education, varied skills, and creative abilities are absolutely necessary for success—both for the individual and for the business. This applies to civilian as well as military ranks. The modern workplace does not need mere managers; it needs leaders who are willing to take risks and will continually develop those entrusted to their care. It is important to practice sound management tactics and skills to ensure the stability of your business, but it is also crucial that you expand your leadership skills to ensure that your Team members succeed as well. You need to know them in order to capitalize on their strengths.

Of the men who graduated BUD/S with me, most were enlisted. Sixty percent of them had bachelor's or associate's degrees, and at least two had master's degrees. One of my classmates had been an electrical engineer for Westinghouse for several years before joining the service. The more you learn about your Team members, the more you will be amazed by the vast pool of knowledge you have to draw from. Review resumes, ask questions, and get to know those you work with. The time you spend learning about your people will yield information that could prove valuable in the future. In years past it was uncommon for an enlisted man to hold a BS or BA, let alone any graduate level degree. If you allow yourself to live by stereotypes and perceptions you will miss so many opportunities to grow and develop a stronger, more cohesive, and more effective Team.

Aside from the fact that individual Team members will know that you are interested in their success and welfare, you will gain a greater understanding of how to best utilize each individual in your Team—which serves to benefit the group as well as the individual team member.

Each SEAL platoon has "departments" to manage the various sets of gear required for the many facets of SEAL missions. The ordnance department handles all issues dealing with bullets, bombs, and weapons. The communications department handles all radios, computers, and ancillary equipment. The air department manages parachutes and rigging and preparation of equipment involved in air operations. Diving maintains and repairs open- and closed circuit diving gear and covers the logistics concerning submerged operations. Intelligence handles information, maps, and cameras. The engineering department handles the Zodiac boats, motors, and other assorted hardware. The two corpsmen comprise the platoon's medical department.

You will be a revered and effective leader if you take the time to find out what drives each member to succeed. With this knowledge, you can assign your people to tasks and missions more efficiently and with the greatest good of the Team in mind. No matter how you hold it to the light, personnel are the Team's greatest assets—and yours individually. Identify those members with a propensity or knack for future assignments or projects. You may have two people who don't like what they are doing and would be thrilled to switch. This simple knowledge can allow you to make the change and produce a stronger, more effective Team. With so many jobs requiring time and specific expertise and skill sets, it is in the Team's best interest to assign to each department those best able to handle the tasks involved. I had a passion for parachuting and aviation, so I was sent to rigger school, jumpmaster school, and other air operations-oriented schools. I headed up the air operations department. It was my charge to pack and repair our parachutes as well as maintain our fast ropes and associated equipment. Platoon riggers are highly trained and are the only men allowed to pack reserve parachutes. To my way of thinking, it would be awfully nice if the rigger actually enjoyed his job. Invariably, every platoon is going to have a "motor head," to which you'll want to entrust your outboard boat engines. The last thing you need ten miles offshore are piles of useless metal that were formerly engines which would serve better as anchors. Every SEAL is responsible for the care and feeding of his own weapons except when it comes to collateral duties, such as those previously mentioned. Each department handles the specifics using their expertise for the good of the Team. Platoon commanders do what they can to accommodate the interests of each individual SEAL; however, it is unrealistic and very restrictive to handcuff yourself to the idea of the perfect fit each time. If you have built a strong team, they will support each other and achieve the stated goals.

People will look up to you and expect more from you simply because of your position and the aura of responsibility associated with your title. Allowing this to get to your head, such as removing yourself from your Team and planning your next career step, will only serve to alienate and blind you. While it is obviously important to plan your own career and account for your own future, avoid the tendency to do this when it is to the detriment of your Team's development.

Get involved and experience the wide-eyed enthusiasm that will greet you when it becomes evident that you are absorbed in and concerned about the Team's well-being and future. I am not suggesting that you invite them to your house every weekend to play with your dog and eat hamburgers. But you must make it evident that one of your duties which you sincerely and willfully undertake is Team custodian. This entails the general maintenance and care of the Team, as well as the "cleaning out" of unsuitable members, if need be! Know who you've got and who you no longer need. Your willingness and ability to identify and remove people who no longer posses the capacity to "play well with others" will be yet another example that you maintain your high standards and hold the health of the team in the highest regard.

Before SEALs go into the field for an operation, the Team is evaluated to ensure the optimum placement of personnel. The officer in charge knows exactly who is going on the mission, what their specialties are, and what roles they will fill. Take a good look at your Team. You need to scrutinize each person and identify his or her strengths and weaknesses, always with the good of the Team, and the individual, in mind. Challenge your members, but do not set individuals or the Team up for failure.

As a leadership tool, maintain a small file on each member. Be open about what you are doing and make it clear that you will be using the information in the file to perform periodic evaluations. These documents must be treated with the greatest of care and responsibility. Keep them in a secure place and ensure that access is strictly limited to those who "need to know." Of course you must also adhere to the Privacy Act and additional rules, written or otherwise, in order to prevent abuse of the documentation. You must set standardized evaluation parameters and continually refine your evaluation system to make it biasfree. Use evaluation sheets to track positive and negative performances.

In the SEAL Teams, the evaluation file is a great tool for leaders, as they rate individual performance against a Navy standard. This helps selection boards make better and more informed decisions about an individual's advancement and future assignments. Within the platoon, the Chief, similar to a foreman, maintains a "training jacket" on all the members of the platoon. This file usually contains, but is not limited to, information about the individual's advancement and performance in specific training and professional development schools. It also contains periodic evaluations and lists the sailor's special qualifications. Other documents track outstanding performance and chronicle trends in performance, be they positive or negative. The latter is crucial if a member proves to be a safety hazard or is just not suited for the job and must be removed. In order to sustain the high quality and integrity of your Team, it is advantageous to maintain a set schedule for reviews and ensure that the evaluation process is executed without bias. In addition, let people know how they are measuring up along the way instead popping the news on them at evaluation time. Give them a chance to prove themselves. You can use an unbiased periodic and active evaluation system to support you decision to terminate those who poison the Team or who have proven through their own actions that they no longer have the capacity to operate as a useful and productive member of the Team.

Often people hesitate to document poor performance because the subject of the evaluation is "a nice person" or has convinced the reviewer that their future performance will be better. But an action that would otherwise be the final straw cannot be, if that is the first time you document performance issues. That is harmful to the individual who did not have the proper impetus to improve their performance or competence, and the organization and the people in it. Now all must suffer through this potentially dangerous fumbling, followed by the pain of termination or even a lawsuit. If the person is that nice or really is determined to improve, they will, and have no further issues. The negative documentation is left to remain alone in a file otherwise filled with glowing reports.

It's also crucial that your evaluation process be objective and detailed enough to be fair to the individuals concerned, in the event that someone other than you needs to utilize the information. Fair, detailed, and objective documentation will also allow the next leader to make informed decisions without re-learning painful lessons themselves, and equip them to do what is best for the Team and the individuals in it.

Moreover, if your Team knows what you are doing and why, as you implement an evaluation and documentation regimen there will be no surprises and they will most likely embrace the system as a way to improve themselves and sharpen their performance. Each member will know that you are serious, and that you are willing to take action in the best interest of the whole.

You must be able to distinguish the difference between a good person and a good operator. In the SEAL community, I have seen men let go to support the common interest. The sailor who is not working well in the platoon or proves that they can no longer be a productive member may be a nice person, but he also may not be appropriate for the job anymore.

Once an individual has demonstrated that they just doesn't grasp the finer points of the job, it can cost your organization a lot of assets; whether it is time, money, machinery or human life. It can cause extra work and irritation for those required to pick up the slack, particularly if the person in question suffers from chronic incompetence, for whatever reason. In the SEAL Teams this person's actions could eventually cost his own or another's life in a training exercise or on a real-world mission. You may be lucky that it is just an expensive piece of gear lost or damaged. Constant evaluation can alert you to negative trends early and afford you the opportunity to pull together and decide whether you can afford to work with and cultivate a "leadership challenge" or whether it makes more sense to find a replacement. The Team has to come first!

To put it this way, you must consider the possible morale issue of keeping a nonperformer. You should track chronic poor performance and take action, even if that means termination, if the situation does not improve over a reasonable period of time. Action, as painful as it can be, will prove to your Team that you are dedicated to the quality of its members and its product or service, and that you will act to preserve the integrity and safety of the Team. Consider the ramifications of allowing a substandard performer to remain a part of your Team. The dedicated members will eventually become fed up and lose faith in your ability to protect the Team. What would be your perception of a leader who you knew had prior knowledge of a performance or safety issue but was unwilling to rectify the situation? If the weak Team member is truly a good person, try to find another job for them. Do not keep them on for fear of hurting their feelings. It will hurt both them and your Team. Sloth and apathy breed rapidly, and if other Team members see that a low level of performance is accepted by the leadership, they will have difficulty producing a high-quality product or service and may soon adopt easier, and likely inferior, standards.

There was a Team Guy I knew who had a problem with situational awareness (SA) in the "kill house," a building in which SEALs practice in-house, close quarters marksman-ship with live ammunition. This is an extremely dangerous exercise, since you are shooting real bullets in confined spaces. The sailor in question repeatedly fired his weapon inches from the faces of his Teammates when it was not appropriate. Other than these isolated infractions, he was a great person and an extremely hard working and industrious Team Guy, always one of the first to arrive and last to leave work. He was always willing to lend a hand to anyone in need. But in the special-warfare business, you cannot afford to be bad at anything. This sailor was given several opportunities to enhance his situational awareness. The first time the training cadre tried to remove him from training was not the first time this had happened. However, since no one had documented the prior infractions, the commander put him back in training, sighting the lack of proper documentation. After he proved yet again that he was unable to maintain the proper awareness in the kill house,he lost his SEAL qualification and was transferred from the Team, this time with a well and fairly documented trend. Although it was hard to see a good man taken down a notch, it did not make sense to wait until someone's parents had to be informed that their son was dead because we didn't want to hurt another sailor's feelings.

The Navy has long selected its finest enlisted personnel to become officers. Choosing officer candidates from the ranks offers several advantages over outside recruitment. First and foremost, the organization has its choice from a pool of personnel who have already made a commitment to the service. They know the organization and have chosen to stay. They are not coming to the Navy green, unsure of what to expect. This is not to say that there are not many advantages to getting a fresh outlook and new ideas from outsiders. However, those whom are already part of the Team know what they are getting into and have a vested interest in its prosperous future. These people know, for the most part, how the organization works. Perhaps the greatest advantage to choosing from existing personnel is access to documentation of their performance according to Navy standards; the Navy's great leadership tool, the periodic, standardized evaluation which provides selection boards with a method to evaluate the potential and worth of officer candidates.

I had been on active duty for about seven years when I seriously started building an officer accession program application package. The Team was about to undergo a change of command. This is the normal and scheduled process in the military, about every eighteen to twenty-two months, when a new officer assumes the reins. The person chosen for the job may already be at your command serving as the executive officer (XO) or he could be from the outside. In this particular case the new Commander was unknown to me. I had spoken at length with the outgoing commanding officer (CO) whom I had worked with for nearly a year about the prospects of becoming a commissioned officer. However, my package would not be complete and ready for submission prior to his departure. The outgoing commander assured me that he would brief the incoming CO about my record, performance, and my desire for a commission. Since the actual submission and review of my package would fall under the incoming CO's time at the helm, he chose not endorse my package as the CO. He explained that it would be more appropriate for the new CO to endorse the package. Two other men from the Team also applied for the same program.

Although we would be competing against applicants drawn from the entire Navy, the CO was required to rank our packages against one another. Two of us were on our way out the door for a seven-month deployment in two weeks, and the packages were due in Pensacola in three weeks. Preparations for deployment are quite detailed and time-consuming, and there are a myriad of family matters to tend to, such as powers of attorney, wills and family visits, because of the upcoming seven-month absence. The new CO interviewed the three of us for about fifteen minutes each. Then we left our application packages with the administration department to await the pending ranking and endorsement by the new CO. At the time of our departure the new CO had not yet made a decision regarding endorsement of any of the candidates.

Once we were overseas, I called my Team to make sure my package had been sent. To my dismay, the new CO had not endorsed any of the three officer-candidate packages. The next day the CO called me overseas to explain that he felt I was a great SEAL but did not yet have enough experience to be a successful officer candidate. With all the diplomacy I could muster, I stated that I was very qualified, in fact an excellent candidate, and that I was competing against fleet sailors without half the qualifications, experience, or intestinal fortitude. He agreed and then gave me his take. I remember gripping the phone with white knuckles as he spoke.

"I know you are an outstanding sailor," he told me, "and will make a great officer, but you are a SEAL under my command. If I am going to put you in for a commission, you are not going to be the best compared to the rest of the Navy, you are a SEAL and you are going to be the best compared to what you and the best of Naval Special Warfare have to offer! You have more potential and I want you to use more of it. If you want to be a naval officer, I want more! I want you to show me that you are ready while you are on this deployment. When you get back to the States, I want you to become a static line jumpmaster and a range safety officer. I want you to take on more responsibility."

I was furious, filled with misunderstanding and adrenaline. I was not accustomed to failure, and this felt like just that…failure. I did, however, have one of the best workouts in a long time after that phone call! I was devastated, what had I done wrong? Later, one of the officers in my platoon pulled me aside and helped me understand the CO's viewpoint and the responsibility inherent in personally recommending someone for a commission. This was a lesson in personnel management and responsibility I shall never forget. I learned that even though you have a strong Team member who is performing beyond expectations, you have to ask: Is that person performing at THEIR best? If you have someone who is excelling and has room to grow, PUSH them to become stronger, smarter, and better prepared for a world that is providing increasingly complex challenges at an extraordinary rate.

While on deployment I worked tirelessly to expand my skill sets. I worked on language and leadership skills. I accepted every opportunity to get outside my comfort zone and challenge myself to become more well-rounded. Just prior to our return home I began submitting the required paperwork to attend both static line jumpmaster and range safety officer (RSO) school. Within the three months following our re-deployment I completed both of the schools.

I was moved into the Team's "training cell," which is basically a platoon within the Team tasked with the responsibility for preparing SEAL platoons for deployment. It was our charge to devise, plan, arrange the logistics for, and set up all the required training areas, transportation, ordnance, and classrooms required to prepare the platoons for each block of training. A month after RSO school, I was in the desert preparing a training scenario for an extremely dynamic and intricate night live-fire exercise for two platoons. Although the respective platoon officers had charge of their platoons, I was ultimately responsible for the safety and flow of the training evolution. The CO would be coming to observe, and

I was still a little bitter and not particularly excited to see him. The CO arrived and watched us complete the scenario setup and demolition preparations for the night's activities. As we walked away to await the platoon's arrival, he caught up to me.

He started off by saying, "I recently signed two qualifications letters with your name on them. The word is that you kicked ass in that last platoon. You did everything I asked of you, and I was wondering if you are still interested in a commission."

At that point everything was clear. My heart rate increased and my mind exploded like the lights at the ballpark after being struck by a homerun hit! I felt about two inches tall for all the misunderstanding and doubt I had harbored for the past year. This man was a genuine and insightful LEADER and a man of true integrity. He hadn't just looked at my qualifications to judge me; he'd tested me to see what I was made of and what more I could offer the Team, in this case meaning our country, and it was now so obvious that he really wanted to "know" me before pushing me to greater adventures. What made me tick? Did I have that extra ounce of resolve necessary to be a naval officer? I had performed well to this point, but had I grown weary and no longer able to accept challenges outside my comfort zone? He tested me to find out, and I will be forever grateful for his true dedication to leadership and his willingness to accept risk.

After the brief moment it took me to collect my thoughts and cool my demeanor I explained that I had already started putting another package together and that I would have it on his desk in two weeks. He gave me a hearty smack on the shoulder, I think he may have grinned, and said he would do everything he could to ensure its success.

Another insight I gleaned from the experience was that we must be the custodians of our Team. Being a Team member means being aggressively proactive in the care and feeding of the group. Take ownership and pride in the Team. Encourage each and every member of the Team to evaluate every situation and continually finds ways to improve. Foster an environment where new and unexpected challenges are met with a zealot's aggression for success. It is smart to reference previous documents and degrees to get a snapshot of each person but you cannot rely on "someone else" to screen and evaluate your Team for you.

This does not mean that you should head-hunt or nitpick. Rather, stay alert for potential problems and stop them as soon as they appear. Know your people. Promote by experience and not by paper. Test, evaluate, and judge.

Promotion should not be simply the result of time spent or checked boxes. Looking back, I wish more COs had the morals, standards, and resolve mine did when it came to deciding whether to endorse my officer-candidate package. If you are involved in the promotion process, you will be judged by the quality of those you recommend and promote.

CHAPTER 2 LESSONS

- Stay involved. How can you learn about your Team if you are aloof and distant?
- Assets. Learn to identify and utilize the talents of those on your Team. Satisfied people are happy people.
- When considering the fate of one, consider the well-being of all.
- Document issues. If it is worth your time to deal with, document it. A thorough and appropriate paper trail can save your butt.
- Identify potential problems before they become critical.
- When you take charge, you become entrusted with and responsible for the welfare and morale of the Team.
- Being a nice person is not a job qualification. Know who your Team members are, what they are interested in, and what they do best.
- Challenge your Team. Break up day-to-day monotony by pushing individual Team members to develop themselves.
- Be the custodian of your Team and encourage others to accept the same responsibility.
- Know and develop; know and remove.

Chapter 3

~~~

Setting the Stage

Challenge Your Team—Mediocrity Is Boring, Unchallenging, and, Ultimately, Demoralizing

As a leader, you must be accountable for the development and direction of your Team. Remember that "Team" is a dynamic term and can encompass any group you choose, from a small work group, the section, the company, the industry in which you work, or the country. Freedom is important and should be granted to all, but if you do not provide direction and stability, the framework and foundation of the Team will falter and crumble. You must provide your Team with the tools and bearing necessary for every individual to make the right decisions, be successful, and develop their future subordinates. Think long-term, act now, and lay the foundation for solid values and growth.

You, as a leader, must set the stage by making perfectly clear what you expect of the Team and every individual in it. Even if you are already established, or have recently joined a new group, you can still set the stage. It requires effort and time to implement any plan, regardless of your resolve, with an existing Team. There must be no gray area in the goals and standards you establish. As the business environment changes, your Team's focus must change and improve, but the direction must always be clear. Set standards high and be honest and open about what they are and how to achieve them. People want to be accepted, and when excellence is the norm, they will perform at that level to be part of the Team.

Inform individual members of your plan and vision for the Team and encourage involvement. It will require the efforts of all to achieve success, so keep everyone in the loop. Call it a vision, mission statement, dream, Team goal—whatever you want; just make sure that your vision for the Team encompasses aspects of your personal leadership plan as well as your Team's direction and goals. What begins as the simple need for companionship will soon develop into a solid work ethic. After setting goals for the Team, let every individual on the Team know what you expect and require from them. Make it clear what will happen if Team principles and individual goals are not met and the consequences that follow. By the same token, praise solid performance and set rewards for such.

Hundreds of men want to be part of the SEAL Teams. Only those who perform at the highest levels achieve the goal. Those unwilling or unable to make the grade or perform as a Team member are released without regret. When you are a proactive leader and part of the best Team around, you will always have a vast pool of interested hard chargers to screen. Be that leader and be the keystone of that Team!

Accountability

Accountability is a central working principle. As a SEAL, when you are culpable for a wrongdoing or mistake, you own up to it and face the consequences. Among the ranks of the Naval Special Warfare community, it is unimaginably worse to be known as seedy and deceitful than to have done wrong and admitted it. Those who are unwilling to accept responsibility for their actions are frowned upon and find themselves either remediated or removed.

Loss of trust and confidence kills a Team and cannot be tolerated. Detect, document, and do away with it. There is neither time nor room for ownerless error in the SEALs, or in any Team for that matter. Deal with situations swiftly and appropriately. Be fair, thorough, and effective in doling out consequences for poor performance and deceitful behavior.

It is futile to encourage and expect people to do the right thing when they know they can get by with mediocre performance or that they can get away with subpar integrity. It is crucial that you make clear that accountability is not only proper but expected, and that anything less is unacceptable and intolerable.

Unless you hold your Team to a high standard, you will invariably receive substandard work, often due to unclear goals, weak discipline, and the lack of direction. When the time comes, you must not hesitate to follow through with your plan. Avoid empty threats; they will eventually undermine your positional authority. Part of setting the stage is carrying out your warnings about the results of indiscretion on the part of one of your people. Failure to do so will undermine your future endeavors and attempts to maintain control of your Team. You will lose that valuable edge required to lead, for you will no longer be holding yourself or your Team accountable.

If you fail to hold those who do not perform to your standard responsible for their actions, your tangible authority will disintegrate. You will cultivate the perception that you are spineless and unwilling to make necessary, if difficult, decisions.

Ownership

As a SEAL, when you are on an exercise or operation, all you have is your gear and your Team. If you take care of your gear, it will take care of you! Instill a sense of ownership of your mission and the equipment you will use to accomplish it. People will be more ambitious and take better care of their tools when they realize that they are responsible for what they are to accomplish, and the equipment or tools required to do so.

SEAL Teams have a decent budget that allows for the purchase of good, serviceable gear. But just because we have the resources doesn't mean that we can treat our gear as disposable. We follow a hierarchy of importance: Team gear, my gear, me! This is an unwritten law.

When we finish any exercise, our first duty is to take care of the Team, or "common," gear. We clean and stow the boats, motors, trucks, parachutes, and any other gear specific to that mission. Two men in each platoon are designated as custodians of each of the various types of gear. This does not mean that they clean and repair it by themselves. Rather, when that type of gear sees use, they take the helm and direct the rest of the platoon in the care and maintenance of it, but every hand pitches in to get it done. If we all use it, we all clean it.

Once the common gear is cared for, we tend to our personal gear: weapons, radios, load-bearing equipment, and dive gear. All is cleaned, repaired, and made ready for the next evolution. Only then do we hit the showers to clean our bodies and put on warm and clean clothes. On rare occasions, some SEALs choose to break this chain. Perhaps they experience just a momentary lapse of reason or the result of poor judgment. The other men, with the Team ethic clear in their minds, make the transgressors well aware of their indiscretion, and usually those in error wind up having to buy the rest of the platoon a case of beer. This is more an example of a social razzing and a way to get someone else to buy the beer, but I am sure you can glean the message from this.

After the gear is properly taken care of, we gather for a de brief to get everybody's input on the goods, bads, and others. This is done with the operation fresh in your mind. We pick it apart and highlight what we do and do not want to repeat. We all take notes of the lessons learned. This is usually done after we put on comfortable clothes and grab something to eat to give the debriefing a more relaxed and productive atmosphere. Okay, so we may have a beer or two as well.

I remember the first time I stood in formation on the beach in Coronado, California, ready for a swimmer inspection by the staff. These inspections happen before every swim as a safety measure, mixed with a bit of structured harassment, to ensure that all the students have properly working safety equipment. The most important points of the inspection are the carbon dioxide-actuated life vest and fixed-blade knife all BUD/S students carry. Salt air and seawater wreak havoc on metal and material, and since SEAL candidates are always in the water while in BUD/S, and for most of our careers, the cleaning and maintenance of all gear is a daily event. That day, the entire class was lined up on the beach, geared up for the weekly two-mile timed swim. Two lines of men faced each other, each man standing across from his swim buddy. All wore a wet suit top and hood, UDT (Underwater Demolition Team) shorts (iconic small brown shorts), a pistol belt with a flare and knife sheath, dive booties, and a UDT life vest with a dive mask stuffed inside it. Each man's fins are stuck in the sand next to him, heel cups wedged together and the blades dug into the sand to form an A shape.

A length of thin orange line attached my mask to my vest, to reduce the possibility of loss in the surf zone. My nose filled with the heavy salt air, and I felt the boom of the crashing waves in my chest. The first instructor to arrive, the corpsman, raced up in the ambulance, a 4x4 Suburban designed to handle the soft beach sand. One student, the class Leading Petty Officer (LPO), yelled, *"Instructor Smith!"* and the entire class responded with a deafening, *"Hoo-yah, Instructor Smith!"* This ritual was repeated as each new instructor arrived. The instructors descended on the students, looking for any faults. As they pored over our gear, the instructor in the ambulance fired up the public address system and asked if anyone wanted to quit. In a monotone voice he said, "You can make the pain stop. Just come over to the ambulance, and I'll give you a warm blanket and a cup of hot cocoa. You don't have to do this. I will help you find your niche in the Navy."

With devious smiles, the other instructors searched our eyes for doubt. They always tried to make us question our ability to pass the pending swim. "Is that all you guys are wearing? That water is cold, I sure hope you don't hype out," one would say, referring to the very real danger of hypothermia. "I hope we picked the right time to coincide with the tide and currents," another might mention, "or at least half the class will fail." Seemingly insignificant comments designed to plant seeds of doubt in your head and challenge your resolve.

One of our duties was to provide the instructors with a surf-observation report. It was a drill to help us learn how to read the ocean. At times they would let us pick the direction of the swim, and then we had to have faith in the men who had prepared the report that day, because their mistake which might result in the entire swim going into the current could cause the entire class to fail.

The formal inspection started, students standing at attention with both hands out, arms bent at the elbow. In my right hand I held the carbon dioxide cartridge for the UDT vest and in the left my perfectly sharp knife. The instructors examined every inch of my gear to see that I had properly maintained it. If they had found corroded areas, tears, or any signs that I had not taken care of my gear, it would have been time to "pay the man." Punishment takes many forms. A favorite is flutter kicks or push-ups until the instructor gets tired of counting. Some of the more annoying involve doing these exercises in the surf, known as getting "wet and sandy" or turning into a "sugar cookie." The packed sand in your shorts and wet suit will cause painful chafing during the ensuing swim.

Some of the instructors had bald spots on their arms where they had tested the edges of countless knives. Keeping knives sharp in Coronado is a difficult task because the salt air and water continuously corrode and deteriorate the edges. That day, one of the instructors became furious because he was finding dull knives. He picked up a rock and yelled, "Okay, gents, if you don't want to sharpen your knives, I will do it for you!" From that point forward, every time he found a less than razor-sharp knife, he smashed the blade on the rock until the blade was flat. The additional hours it took those students to fix the flat blades or procure new knives to replace the broken ones was enough to convince the entire class that the extra few minutes to hone their knife edges perfectly was well worth the time.

Team Concept

I will use the swim to further illustrate the importance of account-ability. At BUD/S, all SEAL candidates must meet certain standards. If the time to beat is thirty minutes, then thirty minutes and one second is failing. After each swim the time for each individual is posted. The failure column frequently lists times mere seconds off the prescribed time. You may be saying to yourself that if someone was only one second off, they should pass; maybe the timing instructor was slow to hit the stopwatch. Maybe? But the standards were fully explained and posted, and if Team members are worried about how fast the instructor moves his thumb, they should swim faster!

During these trying ordeals each man must also rely on his buddy. If one fails, so does the other. Individuals in pairs are not allowed to stray more than six feet from their partners. From day one in Naval Special Warfare, the most important rule is "Never leave your buddy." If the instructors do find a man more than six feet away from his buddy on a swim, he soon finds himself tethered to his partner. The pair must then carry out all their daily activities attached to each other with a six-foot section of mooring line. I am not talking about for a small boat either; this is the stuff that is about ten inches around. This burden is designed to impress upon the Team members the importance of working with part-ners and never leaving someone behind. Not only is leaving a buddy a safety hazard during open-ocean swims, but it also goes against all that SEALs hold sacred.

Teamwork comes into play in almost every SEAL exercise. If some-one's swim buddy is having an off day, the prepared man, or the one who is at a higher level of conditioning or mental readiness, does not have the option of leaving his partner behind and swimming ahead to make sure that he passes the test. The pair passes or fails together. It is each man's responsibility to provide his Teammate with the motivation he needs to pass the time trial. I have seen men drag their buddies through the water to make sure the pair meets the swim time. Every man dares to take it upon himself to do whatever he can to ensure the success of his Team-mates—not only because he might be the one having trouble next time, but also because it is the right thing to do.

In Second Phase, diving phase, the pair concept is taken to another level. Diving operations are inherently dangerous. When you couple this with the clandestine duties of a Frogman, you stack the odds in favor of mishap. That is why SEALs must be physically and mentally conditioned at all times. Every event dealing with dive operations, as well as all others, is handled as the life-and-death matter it is.

When utilizing the Draeger LAR-V, re-breather dive rigs which provide 100 percent oxygen to the diver but are completely closed circuit, the chance of a casualty increases. Although this equipment can be fatal if the operators lose their situational awareness, it is the most clandestine diving equipment available.

The first portion of Second Phase is devoted to educating future SEALs about the proper handling of equipment and the signs of danger for diving operations. In most cases a man and his buddy will have mere seconds to take lifesaving action once signs are recognized. The instructor staff goes to great lengths to impress upon the BUD/S students the mag-nitude of Teamwork while working underwater at night with no light. Deviation from the Naval Special Warfare's strict diving regulations and SOPs is grounds for immediate dismissal from the program.

There is nothing more detestable than someone who leaves a Team-mate in need. This doesn't mean that the strong should coddle the weak and carry them from day to day. Those who are not up to snuff must either be brought up to standard or let go.

If you have anyone in your organization willing to walk away from a Teammate in need, "impress" upon them the necessity to change this attitude. Make sure that being a Team player is part of your mission statement and evaluation system. If the individual in question is unwilling to adopt the Team spirit, cut them and their gangrenous attitude from your Team immediately. Make sure that being a Team player is part of your mission statement and evaluation system. Such individuals are not tolerated on the SEAL Teams. They should not be on yours. This is not only healthy for a designated group but for society. People have become so self-absorbed and we need to break that trend.

There are, however, certain circumstances when individual efforts receive reward, such as timed runs, either on the beach or through the obstacle courses. Though an individual may have already completed the assigned task and may be burdened by exhaustion, he still runs back to encourage those who have not yet finished. This is an act of Teamwork, demonstrated in an evolution geared towards individual effort. For individuals unwilling to participate as Team members, BUD/S instructors have devised a wonderful remedy. They have the individual lounge on the beach as if on vacation without a care in the world as the staff "hammers" the rest of the class in front of them. The individual is forced to sit there in front of his entire class, watching as the instructor staff runs the class through its paces. The deep and sinking feeling of loneliness festers as the individual searches within to determine their level of dedication. Usually within minutes, that person is begging to rejoin the class. To add insult to injury, the lounging classmate is given the bullhorn and instructed to "hammer" the class himself. This is a brutal test for the individual. What is more important? Will you decide that enduring through the pain and suffering, and exhausting every means of supporting the team in the quest for success is greater than your own personal concerns and comforts? After about half an hour of this, the class either has a devout Teammate or one less person.

CHAPTER 3 LESSONS

- Define the following principles briefly, writing a one sentence summary for each one:
- Accountability.
- Ownership.
- Team gear, my gear, me!
- Team concept.
- No ambiguity in mission statement.
- Challenge the Team with high standards.

Chapter 4

The Pragmatic Pedestal

The confident, self-assured, and effective leader is the "quiet professional." These people lead by example and establish credibility by virtue of their own nature. They are positive role models, the kind of people the ranks want to emulate. As a leader your position and power will be greater than that of your Teammates but the image you embody must be realistic and exercised wisely.

Regardless of age, race, or gender, the confident, quiet professional is much more effective and respected than the arrogant figurehead. A bullish and tyrannical businessman may be professionally savvy but is rarely a good leader—and is often an ostentatious blowhard. Businessman is singular. Leader connotes the presence of a Team. Arrogance is not a positive leadership quality. One who attempts to establish credibility and demonstrate greatness by demeaning others in a self-aggrandizing manner only undermines the goals and stability of the mission statement he or she has set forth. The megalomaniac chips away at the stability of the chain of command and stifles a Team that might otherwise achieve great things. Arrogance in the leadership corps serves only to

38

cultivate the type of working environment that is consumed by mistrust and malice, contempt and fear. In this environment, coworkers compete for survival, hoping that they will not be the next to be ridiculed or let go. This type of competition is nonproductive and unhealthy, forcing people to hide deficiencies or looming hazards for fear of blame or admonishment. It is impossible for people to concentrate fully on their work when they dread the presence of the "boss" or the uncertain intentions of their coworkers.

Professionals and businesspeople alike tend to believe that they need to look out only for themselves and not worry about anyone else. They struggle to set themselves apart. Relentless in following their self-centered ambition, they perform for themselves at the expense of others. That's no way to build and nurture a Team. Conceit and self-righteousness have no place. If allowed to exist, these shortcomings will cause the Team to fail. The Team must work together efficiently toward the success of all Team members—through the success of the Team as one unit.

In a SEAL Team, if any man has a problem, the commanding officer wants to know about it. The chain of command must handle the problem at the lowest level possible, but the CO still needs to know the status of his Team members so he can make the right decisions for mission success. Every SEAL, regardless of rank, recognizes the importance of knowing not only whom you've got but what is going on with every part of the Team.

A leader who places himself above the Team may get a bird's eye view of the floor plan but will have little knowledge of the details of the situation there. Once or twice a year, and more often if necessary, the commanding officer of a SEAL Team holds a meeting called a "Captain's call" which is conducted as an open forum. This meeting includes every single member of the SEAL Team and provides an opportunity for anyone to have the CO's ear on any situation or subject he feels inclined to speak about. The commanding officer reserves the right to redirect the question to another Team member better suited to handle the situation, but he is now aware of it and everyone in the rooms knows it and trusts that he will exhaust all reasonable resources to fix the problem if it is found to be valid. There is usually a scribe to take "minutes" so the commanding office can ensure he addresses the issues at hand later on. This record also provides a resource document so he can go back to the person who highlighted the issue for more information or to ensure that the issue has been remedied. This is a time consuming endeavor and he allots a good portion of time in his unrelentingly busy schedule to listen to every member of his Team and address their concerns. Commanding officers who use this tool effectively enjoy the efforts of a supported and motivated Team. Through this process they are able to keep their fingers on the pulse of the Team and are more fully equipped and better informed to handle both current and potential issues.

The most effective officers have learned to manage the relationship between seniors and subordinates. This delicate balance depends largely on the maturity and personality of the Team and its members. If you are in a position of authority, those around you should not need to be reminded of this on a daily basis. Confident and consistent leadership negates the need to reaffirm your position overtly—show, don't tell. The archetypal Special Warfare officer earns respect because he is a staunch protector of his men and a fierce warrior, not a self-absorbed weasel hell-bent on personal gain at the expense of others.

Team leadership has a shelf life. Periodically retrofit your Team's power and authority structure with distinct, unique, and dynamic leadership tactics. You don't need to spend eight months in the mountains seeking divine enlightenment to develop these tactics, and they don't need to be implemented overnight. Expand atop your solid foundation, mission statement, and SOPs, and keep up progressive momentum. Personal leadership flexibility allows you to adapt to any number of work environments and situations. This is your venue for expressing your personality and humanity. Do not become complacent. Never stop developing yourself or your Team!

Among motivated professionals there will always be a natural competitiveness, and this is healthy and fosters development. You have to set the stage for excellence. The entire Team knows what to expect from you and what they should demand from one another. Arrogance and competition for the sake of personal satisfaction only sets the Team leader up for failure. Before long, even the most dedicated and open-minded employees will yearn to see the haughty boss fall flat on his or her face.

It is a rank misconception that the driven, egotistic boss is productive. While work may get done, and good results achieved in the short-term, this style of leadership has long-term detrimental effects on the Team, the business, and the organization. When you are a part of your Team rather than a mere figurehead, and your Team truly supports you, the foundation for success is set and solid. Do not think too highly of yourself. Be a leader and be confident and directed. Let others think highly of you, and let them place you in high regard!

So, as the boss, how important are you? You are in charge, and with that power you have the ability to influence others both within and outside the workplace. This is not to be taken lightly. Your decisions and how you handle situations will reach far beyond the confines of the work-place. To expect everyone in your charge to leave domestic and personal matters at home is neither realistic nor possible; home and work are intertwined mentally. Though some are quite adept at separating the different sections of their lives, the lingering affects remain a factor. To properly deal with a problem, you might have to adversely affect the personal lives of some. But if you become callous and ambivalent toward the personal interests and well-being of those you work with, you will soon find that you have begun an insidious and destructive process. Your cutthroat attitude will create, in your Team members, a perception that you are arrogant. When this happens, you will lose credibility and trust. A chain of command is designed to handle issues, but Team members must know that they can approach you if they need to, and they must be comfortable doing so. Be involved and be successful.

Those who have shown a willingness to use the misfortune of others to get ahead in the SEAL Teams, which is rare to the point of being nearly non-existent, quickly find themselves distrusted and isolated. While this is disturbing for the individual, it also breaks a Team down. Soon everyone is watching his back and those of his buddies and losing concentration on the task at hand. These types of individuals must be identified and quickly be removed from the ranks—to preserve the solid foundation set forth and to keep the Team efficient and successful in its mission and a safe haven for all the remaining members.

If you know you have a propensity to think only of yourself, fix it now! Hiding behind a self-perpetuating sense of personal grandeur is weakness in one of its most insidious forms. Have the courage to change. Don't be "the one" who secures personal remuneration as a result of selfish manipulation of the Team.

As a leader, you need to analyze your leadership tactics and determine whether the power and influence you enjoy have been earned or merely hijacked by the authority granted your position. "Rank has its privileges," we say in the military. And it should. You have put in a lot of time and energy. You have earned the rewards, respect, rights, and privileges of being an upper member of the hierarchy. At the same time, you must accept the increasing responsibility that comes with your achievements. To be an effective leader, you must relish the added responsibility and work as opportunities that arise to help your people become successes in their own right.

Being a leader is a privilege, not a right. If you realize this and act accordingly, you will improve your overall character and that of the work environment. If this isn't your philosophy, then you are in it for the wrong reasons; you must rethink your agenda or you will have a lonely, brief, and unsuccessful stay at the top. Stick with the tried and true, but never stop looking for ways to improve your leadership skills and the business practices you and your company conduct.

Without your Team, you are just a person in charge. You may think you are at the top of the heap, kicking butt and taking names, the operative word being "you." Imagine how much more effective you will be when you begin to work for the best interests of each of your people. If you make it evident that you hold your Team members' advancement and personal and professional interests in high regard, you will find that they will become increasingly loyal and more willing to give you all their energy and they will go that extra mile before you even ask.

During my time in Naval Special Warfare I have worked with men who had the Team concept running through their veins. I'll simply refer to one of the men who made the greatest impact on me by his rank, Chief. Chief began his naval career in the lowest enlisted pay grade and worked his way up to earn a commission as a warrant officer. I worked with him when he was the Leading Chief Petty Officer (LCPO) of my second platoon and I am still close friends with him today.

Chief is an up-front, trustworthy, and reliable leader. He has never flaunted or abused his fortune. You always know where he stands and what he expects. It is always clear that his first priority is his men and their needs, whether personal or professional. He is a busy man, yet he is also the first to lend a hand to the junior men. He wants to make sure each man in his command receives proper training, development, and guidance. The result is that Chief is an extremely credible leader whose ethics span his entire life. I know many successful Team members who attribute their good fortune to his mentorship.

When Chief becomes visibly angry, people move. When he couples that with an order, people move even faster. He so seldom gets angry, and even more rarely expresses it outwardly, because he has built solid respect and a healthy work environment. He does not separate himself from the Team, and he is a working member and mentor. Everyone wants to keep him happy because it seems indecent to perform at any lower level.

Chief is a man I would follow anywhere and without a second of hesitation because I know he holds in high regard my best interest and that of the Team. His men understand that any task he assigns that may be high-risk or result in bodily harm will work out for the greater benefit of the Team. My respect for him is such that if he chooses me to sacrifice for the Team, I will do so gladly with the knowledge that what I am doing has to be done and requires my skills.

As a sign of solidarity and common decency, great leaders will, at times, forgo some of the accoutrements afforded them. If you have been fortunate enough to avoid beginning at the bottom, you must understand how important it is for your Team to know that their leader is concerned about their well-being. If you want an effective Team and greater success, you must make the effort to learn, understand, or experience what each Team member has gone through to get where they are, as well as what they go through in their present position. You will be amazed at the work ethic and productivity of a fully incorporated Team.

I had one commanding officer who would don his combat gear whenever possible and participate in training exercises with his men. Although his duties as CO of a SEAL Team did not call for him to participate in training, he took the time and effort to stay sharp and involved with the Team. He believed, as well, that his men could feed him status reports all day long, but unless he actually got in the mix, he would never truly gauge the climate. This man enjoyed unparalleled respect from his men for his continuous efforts to be part of the process, not merely the figurehead on top. Even though he's no longer in the service, stories are still told of his charisma and strikingly effective leadership.

If you started in the lower ranks, you are due congratulations on your success and advancement. But you should know that you will lose or fail to gain respect unless you always remember where you came from. Promotion must never be about revenge or pursued with soured intent, with the idea that advancement will allow you to get "pay back."

I was selected from the enlisted ranks for a commission. After checking out of my SEAL Team, I arrived in Newport, Rhode Island, for a two-month indoctrination into the officer corps. I was the only SEAL out of the eighty sailors in my class. I had high hopes and expected that I would be working with highly motivated, like-minded personnel who were as dedicated to the Navy and the custody of the enlisted ranks as I was. My vision of being an exceptional officer included the protection, development, and betterment of the enlisted corps, as well as a vigilant assessment of the officer corps.

During our first week in Newport we reported to the uniform shop for our new officer uniforms. It was a great day for me; after nearly ten years of naval service, my dream of earning a commission was close at hand. Similar pride was evident in the faces and actions of my new Teammates as they donned their new uniforms and stood tall for the tailor. Then I heard an utterance that depressed me. "I can't wait to get commissioned and get back to the fleet," a man behind me said. "I can't wait until "Jack" sees who is really in charge, I'll show him." It was plain as day that there really are people out there that desire success in order to demean others.

I turned to the man and said, "If that's why you're here, do us all a favor and get the hell out of here now!" If it were up to me, I would have discharged that guy right there. His sort of self-righteous attitude can only poison and destroy. This man had been part of the program for only a week and already he planned to set himself above everyone else and abuse his power and position.

You must remain steadfast and true to solid leadership principles while being flexible enough to adapt to a wide range of situations without compromising your integrity or the sanctity of your Team. Being a leader takes time and effort, and your capabilities will grow as you progress. You can be satisfied with your current model of tactics as long as you do not allow yourself to become complacent and unambitious in the pursuit of improvement. Keep a constant vigil on how you present yourself. Perception is reality, and your Team can perceive only what they see. Absence begets suspicion; that is why it is so imperative to be involved and visible. Leadership should be fun and fulfilling, so enjoy it, but not at the expense of your Team.

CHAPTER 4 LESSONS

- Do not think too highly of yourself; let others do that for you.
- Enjoy your success; you earned it. But beware of overindulgence.
- Don't forget where you came from if you were once in the trenches. Remain cognizant of the needs of those who are still there.
- If you started on top, do not spend your time patting yourself on the back—that is a waste of valuable time that could be spent developing your subordinates. Create the opportunity to learn the inner workings of your Team. How can you expect to efficiently run a machine if you don't know how it works?
- Have confidence: Be strong, be real, and be trusted.
- Say what needs to be said. If you sugarcoat your thoughts, your message will be lost.
- Absence begets suspicion.

Chapter 5

Have an Open-Door Policy for Opportunity

The way your Team perceives you is reality. Leadership is action and risk. You need to test your intuition and your ideas and act on them. Leadership requires risk in that you must entrust so much of the success of the group to the members of it. It is as dynamic as a shoreline that is pummeled by the surf and carved by the tides. Your leadership style must develop, adapt, and improve. Once you settle on what you think is right or become unwilling or too apathetic to notice the need for change, you become a run-of-the-mill manager, no longer a leader. But if you really want to make a difference, challenge yourself to be a lifelong learner. Your leadership style may already work, and it is important to recognize and use what works. Just make sure that you maintain constant vigilance and are willing to change things when necessary.

Some people have an innate ability to lead, an instinctual charisma. But it is entirely possible to learn, practice, and develop the skills required to become an outstanding leader. It is important to read widely on the topic, observe the leadership styles of others, and ask questions of those you admire and regard as great leaders. If they are worth your admiration, they will most certainly make time to speak with you and help you develop your own tactics.

Your leadership style must be your own, as it is yours to implement. This is not to say that you can't or shouldn't emulate great leaders, but you must add your own personal touch, for you know your group better than anyone else … or least you should endeavor to do so. This is the root of respect and a firm basis on which to build your reputation as an innovative and well-versed leader. You should be sound and solid in your approach but have enough of your own personality woven into the blanket of protection, because that blanket is yet another facet of your leadership. This is the opportunity you have to share your personality with your Team on a professional level.

One of the fastest ways to build resentment is to be a "do as I say" leader. Are you always heard and never seen? Do you demand adherence to standards you are not willing to abide by yourself?

You must assess your actions from the vantage point of your personnel and that of your peers. How would you perceive those actions if undertaken by anyone else? Honest introspection is a powerful tool that has helped me immensely over the years. If your Team acts or reacts uncharacteristically in a situation examine your recent actions before you accuse them of impropriety. This might, and often does, solve the mystery. Your every action and this inventory process must be about the Team! Those who believe in their Teams and are part of them lead great Teams. An outwardly positive and cooperative attitude is infectious. A leader who exemplifies this Team spirit will soon find that he has a group that is united, is interested in success, and can virtually run itself.

Consistency is expected and required from leadership. If drastic change is on the way, your time needs time to prepare for the discomfort. If those in your care think Team is merely a term you use to bolster their spirits, they will be apt to treat it accordingly. The fabric will begin to fray and they may even completely disregard your direction when you need them to overcome adversity and pull together.

One of the main reasons SEAL Teams are so successful is that a close bond exists between the officers and the men. All endure the same training and have a common experience. The officers would never ask the men to do something they would not be willing or able to do themselves. A platoon OIC (officer in charge) shouldn't have to participate in every task in daily platoon life; he has got plenty of work to keep him busy. But he must remain cognizant of the situations his men face and be able to give them direction, and so must you. Think about what you are going to ask your Team to do. Does it make sense? How would you react if you were in their shoes? If the task or tasks seem outlandish and ridiculous, are there other alternatives or solutions?

Avoid the knee-jerk-reaction approaches to problem solving. Consult, cooperate, correct! There will be many times when this luxury is elusive. But when you have the opportunity to deliberate and go over solutions with your people, helping them to come to solutions themselves, take it. It goes back to the old "teach a man to fish" concept.

Often SEAL Teams do not have the time to consider all the options. Decisions need to be made immediately, based on the information at hand. A decision now is better than the best decision made too late. In these moments, your track record with your Team will either hinder or strengthen your authority. If you have a reputation for being dynamic, flexible, fair, and wise, your Team will take the rough spots in stride and back you until the job is completed.

On the other hand, if you are known or perceived to be apathetic, arrogant, aloof, or self-righteous, you will very likely be given only the bare minimum, each person holding back just enough for self-preservation. Your personnel will put forth enough effort to maintain a paycheck as they look for a more fruitful working environment elsewhere. If you have employees who are satisfied with a repressive atmosphere, chances are they are not the top performers you want in the first place. This is why I urge any leader to learn as much about and, if practical, participate in any training their people go through. The more information you have about what your people experience, the deeper the pool of knowledge you can draw upon to make the best decisions possible for all concerned.

An interested and involved leader will breed higher quality followers. People want and need to take pride in great leaders. And they take great pride in being part of a Team led by a dynamic and inspiring person. Be the leader who attracts the best and the brightest. They will have confidence that on your watch their ideas and concerns will be weighed, considered, and implemented if deemed to truly be the correct course of action.

I'm proud that I had the opportunity to work for my last XO as an enlisted man. He was a solid performer and a dead-pan comedian. He had a very calculated demeanor, yet was quick to the draw. He maintained a steady presence in stressful and relaxed settings alike. This man was in tune with the Team and what was going on with every one of the two-hundred-plus men under his care. When other SEALs ask me who I worked with in the past, I take special pride in telling them who and why, and this goes for damn near every SEAL I have worked with.

It seemed that whenever anyone had a problem, he knew about it. The SEAL Team environment is chaotic in that platoons are constantly moving and rarely in town. At any one time, three or four of the sixteen platoon members may be gone receiving advanced skills training. If a SEAL found himself in a bind while detached from his platoon, the XO immediately accepted and shouldered the responsibility of resolving the situation. This involved anything from procuring plane tickets for emergency leave to pay problems, and it always resulted in extended work hours for him. If the situation required him to stick his neck out, he wouldn't punish you if he felt you had learned your lesson; however, he would remind you the next time he saw you in the bar—the price of a pint was well worth it! I know men who have chosen their next duty station based on his presence. This man is still on active duty and maintains the luxury of his unrivaled reputation due to his unwavering adherence to the Team concept.

A "do as I do" leader would not chastise a Team member for taking a smoke break as his very own thumb spins the knurled wheel of a lighter to set ablaze the cigarette he has just put to his lips. These little things have serious ramifications on the morale and structural integrity of a Team.

I served with one officer who was a really good man and an able leader. He really looked out for our platoon. His authority was clear and we were able to flow in and out of social and work scenarios without ever blurring the lines. On the golf course it was first names and at work it was "SIR!" None of the men in the platoon would have ever thought to abuse this relationship because of the solid base he had established since day one. On occasion, however, he would ask his platoon, "Are you guys gonna get any work done today?" as he stood there with a burrito or doughnut in one hand and a coffee cup from the local trend-setting coffee joint in the other. It was always in jest, but when his men were cold, tired, and hungry, they missed the humor. We knew he was a good guy, but our perception at that instance was the reality. Of course we understood this and got over it, I am just saying know when it is time to joke and when it is time to put the coffee down and roll up your sleeves.

The best SEAL officers I've worked with lead from the field, not the sidelines. When there is a difficult task that would benefit from their personal experience, they postpone their other tasks, shed the rank, and teach their men. That time spent with their men often results in many after-hours sessions for these officers, since they must then finish their own work. Even so, they gain better-trained and increasingly loyal men.

If you never take the time to be among your workforce, you will never move beyond the typical us-versus-them scenario. This management environment is designed to let those in charge maintain a touch of anonymity and mystery, which bolsters their ability to control. As a leader, you do not want to control people; you want to convince and guide them. If you are only in control, you have not achieved true success. You push a button and you get the expected result. The scenario you should strive for is to cut the leash and watch your team run!

Great and prolific leaders provide their people with the internal motivation to want to complete the assigned task. When you achieve this as a Team leader, you will experience exponential success. The more autonomous your team is, the more time and brain power are freed up for further development. You have a choice: Do you want your people to provide mindless programmed responses or internally motivated collaborative results?

At times, you may think that your Team possesses the qualities of cooperation, camaraderie, and cohesiveness and yet you are not getting extraordinary results. Examine your situation more closely. If you have camaraderie, is it segregated between workers and managers or divided into cliques? In either case, there is your problem. The spirit of each member working for the good of the others must encompass the entire Team.

During my time in Naval Special Warfare I have had the honor and privilege of working with the most intensely professional men I have ever known. This is not to say that they were inhuman and devoid of personality, quite the contrary. Some of the traits and qualities I consider to be the most important to leadership are flexibility, stamina, reliability, and perspective.

Even so, the three most important words in leadership are consistency, consistency, and consistency. Whether you are the best or the worst leader, happy or morose, friendly or introverted, if you are consistently that, then your people know what to expect and can work with it. A boss whose persona vacillates like the imagination of a child makes for an unsettling, and ultimately ineffective and divisive, work environment. As a leader, you will be required to change and adapt; but you just can't change drastically every ten minutes.

Flexibility, which we will explore in greater detail later, provides you with the ability to handle unexpected situations. It is important to have a plan for possible problems or contingencies. The ability to step outside the box when something unexpected crops up and devise a solution is a powerful leadership tool.

When we speak of stamina as a leadership attribute, it does not mean that you need to be able to jump on the treadmill for an hour and then march another five or six miles. The premise is that when there is a crisis or a leadership challenge, you must be able to see it through to resolution. If a particular situation needs your attention, your Team must know that you will stick with it until it is fixed. If you do have a person who is not operating in the Team's best interest, you must be able to stay strong and collected while handling the issue. If you are mentally weak and break down under stress, your Team will lose faith and confidence in you. This is the beginning of a rapid end.

Reliability is different from consistency. If you say that working this Saturday means that everyone gets next Friday off, you had better deliver. When you say that failure to be punctual carries a prescribed penalty, you must follow through. You will find that when your reliability is on the line, your leadership stamina will be in play as well. Tough, extraordinary times will truly test your mettle and will provide the moments when you will be most closely observed by your Team. Your Team members will be keen to evaluate you and will want to know that their leader is the best and most able. So you must be on your game at all times when you lead a Team.

Perspective is where your intuition and experience will be your greatest asset. If a situation does get out of hand and requires you to remove yourself in order to get a better look, keep your perspective. The ardent maintenance of perspective will prevent knee-jerk reactions that can be devastating because you will tarnish reputation as a calm, cool, and collected problem solver.

My first platoon OIC was among the most dynamic leaders I have worked with. His personality, leadership, and teachings left a lasting impression on me. He was a friend, but during working hours there was no doubt that he was in charge. What he expected from us in cooperation and performance was always crystal clear. He never took advantage of our blind dedication or abused his power. When the work piled up he ditched his computer for a wrench and helped us repair the outboard motors, or perform periodic scheduled maintenance on our dive rigs. He provided a solid and confidential sounding board if you needed help with personal issues. He usually ended with a masculine retort or some other smart ass comment, but that's who he was and we loved him for it. We also never wondered who would take care of us.

Military life is very fluid. When you are at a command, people transfer in and out regularly. SEAL Team sailors form the tightest bonds with their fellow platoon members because they are with those men the most. Although years may pass, old Frogmen don't skip a beat when they see each other once again; all that distance evaporates once they are reunited.

In the Navy, depending upon which warfare community you belong to, you can find out where old Teammates are working. You can get their telephone numbers and e-mail addresses from a database. When I was working on my application package for a commissioning program, I received an e-mail message from my first OIC. About ten minutes later the phone rang, and he was on the line.

It had been at least three years since I had spoken to him. We told a few quick "sea stories" and caught up. We had both been promoted since we'd last met, and the congratulations were plentiful. I began to explain that I was after a commission. Before I'd finished my sentence, he'd offered to write a letter of recommendation.

Then I learned something simple but crucial to leadership. I said that I missed our old platoon and that I'd enjoyed working for him. There was a brief silence. Then he said, with some authority, "No, no, no. . . you didn't work for me. You worked WITH me. We worked TOGETHER!" Okay, so he didn't yell these words but they certainly reverberated in my mind.

I realize that this idea doesn't seem very profound, but it made a huge impact on my life and leadership tactics. It was as if I had insulted him by saying that I had worked for him. He was the epitome of a Team leader. Unfortunately, shortly after he wrote the letter for me he lost his life due to a gear malfunction. We mourn the loss of a friend, brother, and true LEADER. I'd known that in this line of work I would lose friends. But he had not only been a good friend; he'd also been a mentor. His death was particularly hard for me because he was the first Teammate I'd lost. He was that kind of leader, and I will always take pride in the fact that I was one of his men. Since that time and due to more recent conflicts, that number has grown.

Another defining point in my development as a leader occurred on my last assignment before leaving the enlisted ranks. I was deployed with my platoon, and the XO of the NAVSPECWAR Unit to which we were attached was a seasoned veteran with an unparalleled reputation. He had started in the Navy as an E-1, the lowest rank, and worked his way up to Lieutenant Commander.

One of the men in my platoon had slammed the back door of our Navy van, inadvertently shattering the window, so we decided to turn the van in to the motor pool for replacement. The standing rule was that the vehicles were to be kept orderly at all times. It was the rainy season, though, and in our haste to get the van repaired, we turned it in without cleaning out our trash from the previous evening. Meanwhile, the XO, whose many duties included the fiscal health of the unit, decided he wanted to see the damage he was about to pay for.

He was less than thrilled with the state of the vehicle and had a talk with our Chief. The Chief proceeded to read us the riot act for making the platoon look irresponsible and threatened to take away the use of all the vehicles if we couldn't care for them. We knew we should have cleaned it, but we were at a loss to understand the intensity of his anger.

A short while later the XO came to speak with the entire platoon. He sat down and quite calmly stated, "Hey, guys. I am pretty disappointed in how you treated that van. I know accidents happen, but I work hard to get you guys the best transportation I can, and I would hope you would not make me look foolish when I am the one who said you guys deserved to have better vehicles." You should have seen the faces in the room after that simple little speech. A roomful of hardened SEALs hung their heads, embarrassed at having disappointed the XO.

He didn't jump up and down, because he didn't need to. He had set the stage. He was consistent, reliable, and flexible; he could go forever both physically and mentally; and he never forgot where he'd come from. The executive officer always had our best interests in mind, and we all knew it. And now we knew that we had let him down. A broken van window and a few fast-food wrappers do not count as a life-and-death matter, but the way the XO handled the situation was a valuable lesson in leadership. A few calm words from a dynamic, skilled leader who had set the stage for professionalism was all it took to fix the problem and to prevent future occurrences.

On rare occasions a leader can bend the rules and still be great by virtue of charisma. Before I was picked up for my commission I worked in the training cell. The training officer was an intense and unique man. He had started as an enlisted man and at the time held the rank of Lieutenant Junior Grade. He bent the rules because he was a bit arrogant and had a tendency to always be right and know the best way to do the job. He also had a great deal of experience and knowledge. On the rare occasions when he did screw up, all eyes were upon him and everyone was quick to judge. We knew how he was, and his personality was such that he would bounce right back. What made him great was that if you were one of his men and needed help, he turned that same intensity, arrogance, and zeal into unwavering support. He may have been perceived as self-righteous and aloof by those who didn't know him, but his attitude was always geared toward Team success.

CHAPTER 5 LESSONS

- Embody the Team spirit. Lead from the field, not the sidelines. Be like the quarterback, not the coach!

- Take the time to invest in your Team, not your leisure. If you make sure that your Team is trained and motivated, you will be able to concentrate on your work and, in turn, will have free time of your own while they complete their tasks.
- Reinforce the idea that your Team is working with you, not for you.
- Consistency, consistency, consistency.
- Flexibility: Be able to change dynamically when given unique circumstances.
- Stamina: Outlast the issues you face. If you fail to do so, you will fail your Team. When you fail your Team, it will fail.
- Reliability: Be what you say you are going to be and do what you say you are going to do.
- Perspective: Keep it!

Chapter 6

Handling Burnout

Every Team is going to have a different mission and a different barom-eter for success. It follows that your Team members' tolerances for the everyday work of the mission are going to vary from those of other Teams. Factors such as maturity, prior training, personal thresholds, experiences, and personality will be major contributors to each member's drive, initiative, and stamina, for both the physical and the mental aspects of your mission. Anyone stuck in the same routine will wear out eventually. As a Team leader, you need to be able to see the warning signs of burnout and make changes to keep your people interested, energized, and motivated.

The best way to train you to notice the characteristics of burnout is to become a "people watcher," both in and outside of the workplace. Observe and analyze how people interact with one another. Look at different types of body language and how they affect the relationship of the people involved. Be aware that men and women express themselves physically quite differently. This is neither positive, negative, nor even something we need to change. However, it is a facet of human relations we should understand and, in fact, must understand if we want to be effective and productive leaders.

The greatest leaders strive to understand how and why people do things. Knowing these things, they are better able to effect change and glean the most from their Team members. As a leader, you should not coddle your people or wipe their noses after every sniffle. Rather, you should understand why things happen and then determine the best course of action to improve a situation. Avoiding burnout is all about reading your people, analyzing what is going on, viewing as many aspects of an issue as possible, and understanding different perceptions. I challenge you to learn and cultivate a greater understanding of human relations. You will become a better leader.

The Navy SEAL Team is a unique model of human behavior. The Teams consist of the most honorable, dedicated, stoic, competitive, yet Team oriented men I have ever had the pleasure of being around. Every action, goal, and training exercise is a competition and is about beating the other guy, but never to his detriment or that of the Team. Every competitive scenario is geared toward pushing your Teammates to better themselves and to improve the overall quality and effectiveness of the Team.

The manner in which we deal with one another may not be appropriate for all Teams, but the principle upon which our conduct is based does apply. We push one another to excel. We are ardent defenders of morale. The concept of never leaving a man behind is represented in every aspect of our lives. If a man is down in the field, we carry him out. If a man is not performing to his ability, we find out why and what we can do to fix the problem. Our Team is only as strong as the weakest, most inefficient, lowest-performing man.

You determine your own Team standards and expected levels of performance. Your leadership drives the Team, and then the Team will police itself. Peer pressure will drive less motivated individuals to become more productive Team members. A clear and concise mission statement sets a solid standard and makes it possible for you to determine when your people might begin to become overwhelmed.

Burnout occurs for many reasons. An individual can be overworked and exhausted, underworked and not challenged, properly worked but unappreciated. Team members can feel patronized or used. They can feel alone in the crowd or as if they don't fit in with the group, although they may interact well with other Team members. All of this causes stress, which can lead to depression, low morale, and not caring about the mission or the Team. In the end, if you do not have solid standards for performance and are unable to read your crew, they will become worn out and it will be difficult for you to recognize when they are nearing exhaustion. Rapid identification and rectification of problems or difficult situations will serve you, your individual Team members, and the Team well. Catching a problem early will make its solution easier and will send a message to your Team. The time you spend caring for their problems will illustrate to your Team members that you are genuinely interested in their well-being and that you are a hands-on leader. This alone may solve many of your problems, because many inefficiencies and morale problems that can lead to burnout stem from the perception that the leadership does not care about the workforce.

A person continually going that extra mile to complete tasks will suffer from overwork and exhaustion. Sometimes it will be necessary for you to increase the workload near a deadline or for a special project. For the most part, people can and will accept this. But when people who give 110 percent are continually called upon for additional duties, they will burn out. Extra incentives or remuneration can help, but only to a certain extent—you must reach beyond the material and support the intangible. When you take advantage of people and their work ethic, it will become obvious to the Team, even in situations where you give that extra pay or additional time off. The word will spread through the Team, creating misunderstandings or bad feelings. And since perception is reality, until you do something to change that perception, you will be stuck with even bigger problems than meeting deadlines or completing special projects, Regardless of the goal, and whether it's short-or longterm, you must consider the ramifications of the added stresses to your Team members' morale. Chances are that your people will hide their distaste for the continual added responsibility out of duty or loyalty, or because they want or need a good job evaluation or an increase in pay. You should keep an eye on those who do not make a fuss. In the SEALs we understand that a complaining sailor is a happy sailor. Once he stops complaining, he has stopped caring. The caveat is that your Team members must never complain for the sake of complaint, but only to affect some sort of change. Encourage your people to come to you with a quiver full of solutions for the problems they have or see. Encourage unrest, as long as it is constructive.

Often your best employees will work and work, asking for nothing in return. It can be easy to overlook these pillars and take them for granted. But a small effort on your part recognizing jobs well done will pay huge dividends. Most of these performers just want the satisfaction of a productive day or to know that their efforts are noticed. They are not glory hounds, but it is important that they be recognized. Even if they often stay late on their own initiative, thank them each and every time. That is usually enough. You will find that this small action alone can sustain their motivation. If those Team members ever come to you for help, do everything you can within reason to see that they are accommodated.

In my last platoon there was a guy we called HW. He was a big fellow from Hawaii, virtually bulletproof. HW was quiet and professional, and he excelled at everything he did. He was also a solid friend, boundless with humor and camaraderie. While we were on deployment, I was shocked one day to hear him fly into a tirade about something insignificant. Those of us on his Team looked at one another in confusion, then let it go and went about our business. But it happened again about a week later.

That night the platoon got together for drinks in the barracks TV lounge, which we had made into a pub. The unit XO, the same man who had secured the vans for us, had won our right to maintain it, even though the base CO discouraged it. We had built a bar and some shelving, and we'd covered the walls and ceiling with camouflage netting and other Team paraphernalia and memorabilia and dubbed it the Flat Frog.

We were having a great time, but HW was silent. Finally a couple of us began to poke at him. One guy said, "Hey, HW ... what's with you?" Tirade number three! He spoke about the work he had done over the past year or so, the late hours he had put in, and the fact that nobody seemed to notice. Others had been recognized, but not him. After a short silence, our platoon corpsman said, "Thanks, HW." HW looked up, smiled, and said, "Now, was that so hard, guys?" The room erupted in laughter! Case closed. He is still on active duty and has a sterling reputation as an operator and leader. He remains the ruthlessly quiet professional.

That was a powerful lesson. Here was this amazingly hardworking and dedicated Team member. He didn't want an award. He didn't want a raise. He didn't want his picture in the paper. All he wanted was for the platoon to recognize his dedication and for somebody to simply say thanks, and get him a beer.

Overusing your experienced people for the difficult tasks and neglecting to notice and develop your "new people" is a waste of valuable assets. Take the time to train your new people and give them a chance to shine. Don't destroy your best people because everything is an emergency and needs their particular attention. Set up a mentoring program and have the experienced Team members work with the new people and disseminate the knowledge base.

If you always use the same people for the challenging jobs, you will stifle others who want to be challenged. Can you remember how you felt when the teacher always called on the same person? You stopped raising your hand. You stopped contributing, although you may have had better ideas and more drive to learn. The same thing will occur on your Team if you overwork a faithful few and forget your obligations to those not yet experienced. The perception of favoritism will cause resentment. You must never lose sight of the fact that it is your duty to train all your Team members, and part of that training involves developing and placing faith in the "new guys."

The more you push your newer Team members to the side and count on the experience of the seasoned people, the more the new people will lose their motivation. Give them a chance to prove what they can do. When people are involved, they feel important. They have a greater sense of pride, which fosters a more solid and productive work ethic, and one that is contagious.

When people learn that your Team is a place where they can develop, grow, and use their talents, you will draw the best of the lot. When you and your Team are dynamic and successful, people will want to be a part of it.

When I arrived at my first SEAL Team, I, like my fellow "new guys," wanted to get to work as soon as possible. My mind was bursting with new knowledge and tactics, and I was anxious to prove my worth. However, every time we had a high-profile training operation, the "head shed," or Team leader, put it in the hands of the really seasoned guys.

I knew I could go in there and perform, but I couldn't get the chance. How could I become an experienced old guy without experience? I became frustrated. I kept my mouth shut and my ears open, but after a short while I had had enough. I asked to meet with the Chief and OIC, and I mentioned my concerns, explaining that I wanted a chance to prove myself. They said they'd been thinking only of the success of the Team and not my personal ambition. We talked for about thirty minutes before they decided that I would perform a key role in the next operation. I was stoked and popped out of my chair to go get my gear ready. As I left the room, my OIC said, "Hey, you just stuck it out there. If it gets cut off, it's on you ... so don't make us look bad." I understood that I had challenged the decisions he had made and there would be no room for error.

The operation went off without a hitch. I was thrilled, as it was my first important training mission as a SEAL. After the debriefing, the chief approached me and said with a smile, "Thanks for not screwing up." The message was that he was proud of my performance and approved of my tenacity. It felt great to be useful. There are also people who do what is expected of them and perform to the standards you have set. But they feel invisible. The good news is that this is also probably the easiest problem to fix. Save the fanfare for those who exceed the standards. When, however, you have Team members who have been with you for a while, who are present and on time every day, and who do their jobs to the standards you have set, make sure you notice them. If you have a company newsletter, thank them in it, or give them an extra day off; there are any number of suitable rewards that say, "I appreciate your efforts. You are a welcome and valuable member of the Team."

One of the worst feelings as a Team member is that your contributions and efforts are for naught. When you assign someone a task, empower them sufficiently so that they can complete it. If you trust them enough to make it theirs, let it be theirs—unless, of course, they are going to get somebody hurt. Burnout from frustration is a very real threat, and recovery from it is hard.

Mentoring is a powerful tool when properly implemented and monitored. If you are going to use your hot runners to train the new people or the non-performers, let them do so the way they see fit. People will burn out faster when they feel they can't put forth their best efforts or will be constantly checked. After all, you delegated the task to them because they are closer to the situation and have a better working knowledge of its intricacies. Don't put your best assets in a position to fail. Don't let them perceive that they are failing. Many people have personal standards unique to them and it can be very damaging if those standards are not satisfied. You cannot task someone with improving the non-performers, then tie their hands and make them incapable of reaching their own goals, or effecting any real change or improvement.

As I mentioned, before I started the ROTC program, I spent two months in Newport, Rhode Island, for an indoctrination course. I was dissatisfied with the physical fitness level of the majority of the other officer candidates. By Navy standards, the majority passed, but just barely. I was appalled by the number of officer candidates who allowed themselves to perform so close to the minimum. If you are going to be in front, you need to be worthy of that position in every way. I wasn't satisfied with the intensity of the three mandatory physical fitness sessions I was required to attend per week, so I offered to run them. In addition, I volunteered my time to run the extra P.T. (physical training) sessions, required for those who had failed the physical readiness test (PRT) or were over their body-fat limits.

My superiors agreed, and I had the class for two months before the next PRT. I made a plan to run them hard but smart. I explained that I wouldn't have them do any physically damaging exercises, and I promised that if they gave me their best effort, I would improve their conditioning. A healthy body, I said, creates and supports a sharper mind. I offered after-hours time to those who wanted nutritional advice or one-on-one P.T. help.

In the beginning, many of my classmates couldn't do all I asked of them. I told them that it was better to do what they could correctly than to do all the exercises improperly. A couple of weeks into the program a few people complained to the staff that I was being too hard on them. They said that they weren't SEALs and I shouldn't demand so much from them. I explained to the staff that the sessions I conducted weren't as rigorous as those I'd experienced as a SEAL. Furthermore, my goal was the vast improvement anddevelopment of both their bodies and their knowledge of fitness.

Still, I was ordered to reduce the intensity of the workouts. I was furious! I had spent my own off time to improve the class. Now I was being told to dial back because a few of my classmates felt I'd set the bar too high. At the next session, I was handed a script. I looked it over and asked, "This is just the warm-up, right?" I was appalled by the low standards. Many of my classmates had told me enthusiastic stories about how they hadn't felt so good in years due to the previous workouts; now I was ordered to lower the bar.

I explained to the staff that I was getting results and said that I found it sickening that the entire class should lower themselves to the level of the unmotivated and weak. Nevertheless, I was asked to stick with the script. I did not want to undermine the staff, but after two sessions of the "new" program, I'd had enough. People were unaware that I was ordered to alter the workouts and asked what was wrong and why had I made them so easy. The disappointment was obvious in the faces of the majority of the class, who had realized for the first time in their lives that they could really push themselves. I went to the staff to get them to change their minds and put me in control again. They refused, and I offered to step down, being unwilling to support mediocrity. They asked me to stay in my position, and I did so with the hope that they would soon see my point.

Near the beginning, we had run in the snow, freezing rain, and sleet. While everyone else bundled up, I ran in shorts and a T-shirt to prove that mental power was crucial, and soaking wet sweatpants and sweatshirts get really heavy and uncomfortable. One day, we were on a 2.5-mile run in mixed rain and snow. The frigid wind off the sound cut right through our wet clothes. I could not stand the political bickering about the workouts anymore and found myself unable to support the head shed's apathy, so I ran among the men chanting, "If it doesn't suck, we don't do it!" That, coupled with an occasional overenthusiastic, "Yeah yeah yeaahhhh," started to fend off the cold. Soon the class was echoing these utterances. This kind of motivation is contagious, and by the end everyone was joking and "reminiscing" about the toils of the run they had completed just some five minutes prior. Attitudes were changing. Once we were back in the gym, I told the class that something easy never makes a good story.

Soon, the majority of the class started to jeer me for making the P.T.s too easy. The spirit of Team competition had taken over. The class began to demand more from one another and from me.

You want this to happen. You want the Team to delegate the task of morale management to themselves. The class I led now had internalized a much higher standard, and it was blatantly obvious in their performance. I cranked up the P.T.s to even higher levels than before. And the class loved it! The gym filled with motivated taunts and yells for more pain. For the next few weeks we trained like animals, and the staff never said a word. When the class took the final PRT, the numbers of pushups and sit-ups had skyrocketed.

Run times had dropped by minutes for each person. Only one person had never joined the Team. He'd remained a lone individual and stayed out of shape. He had never come to me for help or advice. In fact, I'd told him halfway through that I did not feel he belonged, that his heart wasn't in it. He said they wouldn't kick him out after he'd made it this far. Indeed, the staff had considered waiving his requirements so that he could graduate from the program. But the rest of the class was outraged. They had all worked their butts off and earned their scores, now they were seeing that it didn't matter. I approached the staff and conveyed the sentiments of the Team. The failing man was dropped from the program the next day.

If your people begin to reach burnout when completing normal duties, look for other problems: illness, troubles at home, not being suited for the job. If the entire Team approaches burnout, are your standards too high? An engine is designed to propel a car, but if you stress it, it will break.

Rewards can be a very powerful tool; use them as such if necessary. Rewards are important. Your rewards will be unique to your situation and resources. If you can give a raise or bonus, do so. If you can give some sort of meaningful award, do so. Whatever you do, it must be sincere. Empty thanks and token awards do more damage than good. Find out what people want, and remember that not everyone will respond the same way to every reward. Be original; think of something new.

Set your standards high and let the crew do the work. When your Team sets high standards for itself and expects that level of performance from all of its members, don't deflate their morale and motivation by coddling the non-performers and the weak. What message do you want to send your people? When you expect the best from them and most of them deliver, don't accept anything less than that from the others. If your people see you accepting mediocre effort from an individual, you will lose credibility and power. Maintain a constant vigil and be flexible enough to adapt and develop with them.

CHAPTER 6 LESSONS

- Be a student of human interaction.
- Do not take advantage of your Team!
- Burnout will engender low morale.
- Be mindful of your Team's morale level.
- Identify and quench burnout before it happens.
- Motivate your Team to be the custodian of its own morale.
- Know your people and their personal standards; deviation from those standards may indicate a looming or manifested problem.
- False or petty rewards can often do more damage than good.

Chapter 7

~~⌒~~

Flexibly Inflexible

When I arrived in southern California to attend BUD/S, I was in great physical condition. I had been running, swimming, and lifting almost every day of the week. My very first physical evolution at BUD/S was a four-mile, soft-sand conditioning run. I had been training in soft sand and felt that I was well prepared for the task. However, by the second mile of this instructorled run, I was sucking wind like never before and attracting the concern of a couple of the instructors.

After a few weeks of this, my class proctor, the instructor in charge of the class, approached me. He explained that he could tell I was giving 110 percent, but that I was unable to stay with the front of the pack because I was running wrong. I gave him a puzzled look. I had played sports my entire life and thought that I was a good runner. He took the time to show me how to run properly, which was very uncomfortable at first. My entire life I had run with my arms pumping vigorously by my sides. He explained that all this did was tighten up my chest, restricting both its expansion and my oxygen-uptake efficiency. The revised technique was to let my arms relax by my sides with very little back and forth movement

ment. If you run like I used to, try this new arm style. It took me several weeks to adapt and accept this change, but it made all the difference in the world. The lesson I learned is that what seems comfortable now may not always be the best or most effective way.

Flexibility is one of the major qualities required to cross over from the old managerial paradigm to the dynamic, fulfilling, and challenging environment of a Team leader. Nothing is absolute, and you must be ready to adjust when the need arises. It is when you leave the confines of archaic and restrictive thinking that you begin to recognize hidden potential in both your subordinates and yourself. You must develop a sense for what is and is not an acceptable level of deviation from the expected tier of performance.

Inflexibility is tantamount to stagnation, which is not conducive to progress. The ability to adapt and bring your Team with you is one of the traits of a great leader. Although I advocate flexibility, this in no way means that you should ever compromise your standards; that is where it pays to remain inflexible.

Do not fear change. For some, this will be hard to accept, because it requires departure from the traditional model of management, where ideas about people, their duties, and the roles of the leader are fixed. In military school and boot camp I was taught to do what I was told, when I was told, and nothing else but what I was told, no questions asked. This is all well and good if you have a huge force of people to move, control, or direct to lead in the completion of a task. But if you treat your handpicked professionals like mindless sheep, you will soon find yourself left with just that: a bunch of disgruntled, moderately productive sheep. You will not reap the benefits of a stimulated and fulfilled staff. Excessive supervision and control leads to micromanagement, a debilitating menace. You should not be flexing your authority and coercing others to do your bidding. You should be working with them for the benefit of each individual and for the good of the Team itself. To be effective in a dynamic situation, you must be ready and willing to deviate from your comfortable norm when that's what's required to successfully complete the task.

If your crew consists of twelve people, you will have the advantage of twelve perspectives. Capitalize on this diversity. If you remain aloof and unapproachable, you will remain alone and un-approached. The entire purpose of leadership is to effect change through the organized efforts and collaboration of the whole, rather than the direction of one, as in the typical management paradigm.

The size of your organization will dictate the amount and quality of the contact you have with each person. This is where you must consider the ramifications of an effective chain of command. This is where it is paramount that you instill the solid leadership foundations in your immediate staff so they can in turn lead those in their care. When well organized and developed, this actually allows you to be closer to a larger number of people by virtue of the standards and environment you have built. Be who you want your subordinates to be. The way you treat your Team of leaders will affect how those people treat their workers. When you set the example of being flexible and willing to adapt, your attitude will filter through the organization. Reap your rewards by making it known that everyone is welcome and expected to proffer new ideas and suggestions. At the same time, institute a policy of "No complaints without solutions." This will help eliminate frivolous griping and will force your personnel to think critically and creatively to solve problems on their own. Ultimately, your employees will become more involved and conscientious.

You cannot plan for every scenario ahead of time. What you must do when approaching a situation is review lessons learned from previous events and situations, formulate a collaborative plan for action based on the Team's goals, and put the plan up for scrutiny. Then, time permitting, tear it apart, look for holes, and plug them with contingency plans.

Few of us enjoy an abundance of time. We must maximize every second. The beauty of reviewing lessons learned is that they allow you to narrow the focus and scope of the what-ifs. What went wrong last time, and why? How was the situation resolved before? Was that the best way to fix it, or can we do better if it happens again? You need to ask these questions before, during, and after any situation.

Be wary of complacency because it ruins morale; it will end up disrupting the flow you have established and undermine the desired end state. In the SEALs, complacency can kill, literally. On the professional level, complacency can allow the Team to become inefficient, consumed by internal and external competition, and subject Team members to burnout, another fatal group dynamic disease.

It is imperative to have a well-thought-through and practiced plan for action. Open your mind and remain one step ahead of potential problems. When encountering a problem, you must be willing to reassess the situation and decide whether to continue as planned or take a new course of action.

I have been in situations that have ended undesirably when seasoned veterans were unwilling to accept new ideas. They argued, "This is how we did it in my last three platoons." But what worked well then didn't work this time. In situations like this, evaluate what happened and record lessons learned for next time. Rely on the experience of your seasoned Team members. Remember that just because someone is new or junior does not mean that they cannot have a great idea or solution to a problem. Pull from as many resources as time allows; consider your options, then act.

Do not asphyxiate your achievers by closing them out in times of crisis. There will be cases when there is not enough time, nor is it a good idea, to consult everyone and consider their thoughts. But when you do have the time, take it! Allow them to be part of the solution. It is dangerous and foolish to close them out. When your people stop coming up with ideas or different ways to do things, that is when you need to be concerned. You have either shut them out or killed their morale. Keep innovation alive.

In addition to contingencies, SEALs always develop a set of "Go" and "No go" criteria before embarking on any operation. The final call is always made on the scene, and, to minimize the errors of judgment inherent to crisis situations, is based on a solid set of criteria established beforehand. Predetermined criteria are an aid, but we must still be able to analyze and adapt on the spot. We look at what it will take to complete a mission, the importance of the mission, and the minimum assets required. What if certain equipment is damaged during insertion, will that compromise the ability to complete the mission? What is the maximum number of casualties or injuries the Team can sustain before the operation is no longer feasible? Is there a certain time, after which it will be too late to get the job done?

If it is at all possible to rehearse a plan, speech, presentation, or procedure, rehearse it. In the SEALs we will plan a mission similar to what we have done many times before, but we will always rehearse the current plan. Repetition breeds familiarity, and once you know a situation, you can analyze it better. Flexibility plays a major role in this process as well. If you are on your last practice run and you find a flaw, you must have the discipline to stop, analyze the plan, and change it if necessary. The rehearsal process must start over, but when the operation goes off without a hitch, it is well worth the time. The first time you execute your plan should not be during the actual situation. It is imperative to factor in time for rehearsals and review. Make the mistakes in the comfort of your Teamwork space or office, where the situation can be controlled and modified, not in the field, where it may be too late.

Another facet of flexibility is the willingness to allow your people to make mistakes. Nobody is perfect, not any of us. The mistakes we make, and how we handle and learn from them, define who we are. Do you wallow in a quagmire of self-pity and remorse, or do you analyze what went wrong, reformulate your plan of attack, and reassert yourself?

If you maintain a log of lessons learned and use mentoring to ensure effective information dissemination, you will be less likely to encounter problems. If your people are making mistakes, however, it means they are trying. If they make more mistakes later, it means they have enough drive and personal motivation to brush themselves off and try again.

That is perseverance, and that is what you want. The important factor to remember is that if they continually make the same mistakes, there are other issues at hand that must be resolved. If they are bracketing and making smaller and smaller mistakes that are rapidly approaching the desired result, let them grow.

If no one on your Team makes mistakes, you are either the luckiest leader in the world or your people are so afraid of collapse (or of you) that they are unwilling to risk failing and the ensuing harsh consequences. They may be holding back and producing "safe" but not fully developed solutions and ideas. You want dreamers and risk takers who are striving to improve, who are willing to make mistakes along the way, learn from them, and continue on. This process, of course, must withstand the test of reasonableness. When a person is intent on success, it is both possible and probable that they will fall on their face a few times. Record the lessons learned, reevaluate, and re-attack.

All too often people are unwilling to let others develop. At the first sign of trouble or the first stumble, they don their cape and race to the rescue. Unless it is a life-threatening situation, all this does is frustrate and demoralize the individual and, ultimately, the Team. How will it be possible for your subordinates to realize the consequences of their mistakes, personal and professional, if the over controlling manager intervenes every time any difficulty arises? Everyone must be held accountable for their actions, but at the same time provisions should be made to accommodate the learning process.

There will be times when you have to discipline people who have strayed beyond the confines of good order that you have set forth. That, too, is a part of leadership. If disciplinary action is to be taken for a mistake, let it also be known that extra efforts are noticed and appreciated. When all the members of your group understand that they are allowed to make mistakes if they do so with honorable intentions but will be held accountable nonetheless, they will focus their efforts. They will still take risks in the interest of advancement but with greater reverence and care.

From day one of BUD/S training with your operational SEAL platoon, the instructors drill into your head that you must train the way you fight. It is always real, since 90 percent of the training we conduct uses live bullets and explosives. There is always a chance that someone may be seriously injured or killed.

When I was on my first SEAL Team, I had the opportunity to attend the Naval Special Warfare scout sniper course. I had graduated BUD/S almost two years prior and had been working like crazy ever since. I had learned to take every training exercise seriously and treat it as if it were the real thing. A very close friend of mine told me the following story which occurred during his time at the same school. I will add explanations where needed. When he told me the story, I was about to start the course. He wanted me to learn from his mistakes; passing on his lesson learned.

One day in sniper school, I was on a patrolling and reconnaissance exercise. I had done what seemed to be two hundred of these missions already, and I was tired. At dusk, I was approaching the suspected target area. In the SEALs, we recognize a prescribed distance around a target as a hostile area. I was well within this domain for this operation.

In these situations, SEALs are supposed to be extra sensitive to their surroundings, taking in every chirp of a bird or rustle of a leaf. We walk slowly, allowing our senses to adapt to the environment, analyzing light and abnormal tree shapes. We calculate every step for pressure, noise, and print left behind. Scents carried on the wind can make your spine tingle, like when you smell the smoldering fire at the target sight. Your rifle is a split second from its place at your shoulder, your thumb ready to deactivate the safety, your trigger finger poised on the trigger guard, ready to slip into place. Your eyes are wide and your mouth slightly open, to receive that extra bit of sound. Eliminating one sense heightens the others. Every couple of meters you stop to scan; then you close your eyes momentarily to heighten your listening senses.

There I was, within five hundred meters of the target, my stance erect and my rifle by my side in my right hand... not ready to go at all! I had relaxed my posture because of fatigue, and at that moment I learned that in the game of war, the second you let your guard down, your enemy will kill you. I took two more steps and looked up. Twenty meters ahead of me, standing in the middle of the trail, was one of my instructors, arms folded across his chest, head shaking in disappointment. I had not seen him. This was not because he was hidden at all; in fact, he was standing in the open. The low light coupled with my lack of attention allowed me to get that close before noticing him. I looked at him for a second or two, gathered myself, and got back into the scenario, adopting the techniques of stealth taught by the instructors. I immediately stepped into my heightened senses, melted into the forest, and continued on my way as if the incident had not taken place. This was not the time to reflect on my mistake; it was the time to concern myself wholly with the job at hand and to complete it to the utmost of my ability. There would be time to lament later.

After every operation, training or real, we have a comprehensive debriefing to identify both good and bad points. This is a time when all is laid out and nothing is personal. Everything that comes up is mentioned strictly to improve the Team and to prevent such a mistake from happening again. The instructor who saw me never mentioned it to anyone, and we have never discussed it. He made a judgment call. He chose not to bring up my indiscretion to the class. Had it not been for my track record, I believe I would have been kicked out of the school, but this man stepped outside of the box and realized that his piercing gaze of disappointment was all the reprimand I needed. Another instructor might have seen only right and wrong and made the situation public, but this one did not. I had made a mistake, and we both knew it. In a real-world scenario, this same mistake could get me or my platoon mates killed. In that brief moment of unspoken counseling, I decided, and he knew, that I would never let my professionalism wane again. Until now there were only two individuals that knew of this event, which has haunted me every day since it occurred.

He told me the story because he trusted me and never wanted me to let my guard down. What if the first time you do is in combat instead of training? This was never going to happen to me. I reflect on this story often whenever I feel my senses begin to dull.

Successful leaders do not fit into one mold. Leadership, by its very nature, is an entity of change and diversity. The great difference between a leader and a manager is that the leader has the courage and takes the latitude to stray from the norm, develop a vision, share the vision, and go after that vision together with the Team. As a leader, you will be required to handle everything from strictly business situations to the intricacies of the personal lives of your Team members. You must be ready and able to approach these issues with the guidance, assistance, and support of your entire group.

If you are a staunch subscriber to the outdated management model of achieving common goals, you may survive but will lose untold wealth, both monetary and human. You must be involved and concern yourself with the Team's concerns. If you are cognizant and flexible, you will avoid desperation and knee-jerk reactions. When you function as a cohesive unit—collaborate, rehearse, and attend to lessons learned—you will enjoy greater success.

As I mentioned earlier I was in the training cell of one of my SEAL Teams. I had been teaching the land warfare tactics passed down through the years. After the twin towersowers came down, the world changed forever. Soon SEALs were deploying and engaging this new enemy. One of the platoons I had put through training returned from combat in Afghanistan. It was great to see them and hear their stories. One of my first questions to the OIC of the platoon was whether the tactics we had been teaching worked. He looked at me for a moment, and then with a quizzical expression, said, "No." In fact, he stated they had to pretty much reinvent new tactics on the fly in the heat of each engagement. It was a little painful to realize that what I had been telling guys to do was no longer valid, but it was a good lesson.

CHAPTER 7 LESSONS

- Allow people to make mistakes; that is how we learn.
- The way a person handles and learns from a mistake helps define them.
- Before taking action against someone who has made a mistake, carefully consider whether it was done with malice aforethought, was the result of carelessness, or was simply an honest mistake.
- If you rush in to remedy a mistake before the consequences are apparent, your people will become complacent and rely on you to fix everything.
- Let your Team members learn and develop.
- Avoid knee-jerk reactions.
- Practice accountability and encouragement. Hold people accountable for their actions, yet do not be so overbearing as to stifle their future efforts.
- Remain dynamic and aggressive with regards to change and flexibility, but never at the expense of the Team, its goals, or its high standards.

Chapter 8

The Menace of Micromanagement

If you know everything, you just might get the opportunity to prove it when everyone leaves you to it! A leader knows when to be hands-off and let the machine function, and when to get in the mix and lead. You are part of a Team, and letting go and letting those you trust function on their own may be one of the most difficult balancing acts you will ever perform. If you give a competent individual or group a task and empower them to accomplish it, you must accept the results, unless they adversely affect your goal. In order for this process to work you must make your expectations clear. As previously stated, you can't expect people to read your mind and if there are a specific set of parameters required for success, let them know ahead of time instead of popping in on them after them have already produced results.

The only good thing about micromanagement is that it can be fixed. Be wary of the impulse to micromanage and be sure to accept new ways of doing things if the results will accomplish the common goal, even if they aren't what you initially had in mind. Do not make your Team revisit work because they didn't do it the way you had learned to do it. Have faith in their experience and own creative thinking.

When you delegate projects and allow the process to function as you have designed, you will benefit from different perspectives on dealing with situations and on reaching goals and you will gain insight into the individuals who make up your Team. If you continually second-guess and change the work of your subordinates, not only will you kill their morale and motivation, but you will create extra work for yourself. Successful leaders let their people do their jobs and concentrate on their own work. This is more than effective time management; it is an inspiring use of resources.

Set up your environment for success. When you are preparing to delegate a task, take the time to consider your options. Make sure that you choose the right person or people for the job and that you are not setting them up for failure. You will have to know whom you've got, what their talents are, and what their current workload is. Once you have this information, explain the key points or details of the tasks at hand and the objectives, or goals, of the work. Do not assume that your Team members know these from the outset. If the project is important enough to be done to exacting specifications, take the time to explain these details. Clarification of particulars in advance is professional guidance. Chastising innovation, which happens in the absence of professional guidance, is professional suicide.

If you have fully explained the parameters of a given task and the result is not what you had intended, you must find out whether it was a misunderstanding, bad intentions, or a lack of attention that caused the inconsistencies. At this point you have two options. You can explain the pertinent details again, point out the flaws, and let your Team try again; or you can take the time to mentor and show them what you expected. Either way, you must analyze the situation carefully before chastising them. Did you do your part and give them the information they needed?

You lose credibility if you expect others to be mind readers, then reprimand them when it turns out they don't have that skill.

One of the most damaging types of micromanager is the control freak. This is the person who feels compelled to control every situation. People with this flaw force their opinions on others, even when they are not experts in the subject at hand. You must be able to recognize this tendency in yourself or your subordinates. Once you recognize it, you must fix it. Many micromanagers lack confidence and feel that they must be the center of attention and the keeper of knowledge to maintain respect. Some of these people lack the ability to trust others or simply do not want to share the glory of a job well done. Just because you are in charge does not mean that everyone is going to expect you to know everything. That is what the expertise of the group as a whole and the talents of the individuals are for. You must have a working knowledge of the operations. But it is not possible for you to maintain intimate knowledge of every task required for carrying those operations out.

If you are reluctant to trust or let go, you must learn. Think of the added time you will have to complete those tasks that are truly yours.

Some micromanagers like to interfere with their subordinates for personal gain. This sort of person knows the power of information and tries to maintain a monopoly on it. They hold back key knowledge, keeping it to themselves, and only produce it when it will benefit them. This behavior is a sure morale killer.

As a competent leader, you must always put the well being of the Team first. Successes and failures are a group experience because each member is involved. If you are willing to shine and leave your Team behind, you do not belong in power.

The key to Navy SEAL success is that SEALs never leave a Teammate behind. Never! Amongst your group, every member must be included in the Team's successes and rewards. As a Team leader, it is your responsibility to motivate those who aren't top performers. If you or any of your

Team members are thinking only of themselves, the result will be the devastation of morale.

In all my time as a SEAL I have seen only one person who I felt truly missed the mark as a leader. Everybody has his or her moments, but for this person it seemed to be a lifestyle.

One night in the southern California desert, I was the point man leading my platoon on a training mission. The point man usually carries the lightest load because he is supposed to scout ahead to determine the ideal path and spot any booby traps. The patrol order was as follows: point man, officer in charge (OIC), radioman, M-60 gunner, medic, M-60 gunner, leading petty officer (LPO), and rear security man. As the point man, my sole purpose was to select and navigate the safest route into and out of the target area. In addition, it was my responsibility to ensure that the men rested and the Team's pace accommodated the heavily laden M-60 gunners. To do this, I needed to find suitable resting spots during my probes forward. The "Pig Gunners" (M-60's) and Comm Guys carry quite a substantial load and require periodic breaks to stay fresh.

According to the scenario parameters for this particular exercise, global positioning system (GPS) units were considered inoperative because the notional enemy had knocked out the GPS satellites. But I rarely used the GPS units anyway, as I always relied on my map, compass, pace count, and terrain features. With these tools I could determine how far it was to important landmarks and reset points. In addition, I kept navigation information in my head; we were always instructed not to write it down, in case we dropped it or were captured. Another drawback to GPS units is that they store route information and could provide damaging intelligence if they were to fall into enemy hands.

It was standard operating procedure for our platoon that the point man be the forward eyes and ears. You can't just plop sixteen men down in hostile territory. You need to find an area that will conceal them and provide cover and defensive positions. I took pride in being able to balance these duties. Those heavily burdened needed breaks, and I found a spot every few hundred meters. Of course, this was great for me as well, since I could separate myself and listen without the noise of the men.

The OIC was a smart and educated man with years of military service. He was adept at handling the daily paperwork and had just about every bit of military lingo and tactics committed to memory and knew when to use it. I was not particularly fond of his management tactics, but I'd left my personal feelings back in the barracks. I liked and needed the space in front to analyze the terrain and make good decisions. On this night, however, my OIC was never more than four feet behind me. I asked him several times to stand off, because all I could hear was the crunch of his boots against the rocks. But a minute later he would be on my heels again. Then he started asking me where my GPS was and if I knew where I was. I responded that GPS units "didn't work" here according to the provided scenario and that I knew exactly where I was.

Frustration started to set in. I was thinking, "He picked me for the job because he knew I could do it well; now he's riding my ass and hindering my work." During our next break he asked me where we were yet again. I pulled out my poncho and covered our heads and the map. I produced a subdued red-lens flashlight and pointed out on the map where we were. Then he asked for an eight-digit grid coordinate.

While I was checking the grid, he was fiddling with his personal GPS. I looked at him and said, "Sir, GPSs don't work, remember?" He just looked at me and asked for the grid again. I gave him a quick grid from the large-scale map. We were in the middle of the desert in featureless terrain. I was recording our position by pace and bearing, and we were already several thousand meters into our trek. I knew where we were and where we needed to go. Then he asked if I wanted to know where we really were. I was fifteen meters off according to his GPS, even though it was tracking only two satellites at the time, which could result in reduced accuracy.

We continued, and I did everything I could to ease my frustration. Then he started telling me where to stop for breaks. I explained that I knew from my premission map study there was a wash ahead big enough to house the entire platoon, but he wanted to stop where we were, and we did, in the open, with the entire platoon exposed. I crawled around to each guy to make sure my pace was good for all. A few of the guys looked at me in disbelief and asked why I had left them so exposed for our break. I explained briefly, and they understood.

We started patrolling again and, twenty meters later, we came upon the huge wash I had seen in my mission prep. I dealt with the OIC's micromanaging, knowing the Chief would straighten the situation all out when we returned. There were several times, however, when I wanted to invite him to lead the patrol. It would have been great to see him fail. He couldn't have known the navigation plan as I did, because I was the one who'd planned it.

By the end of the night it had become blatantly obvious that the OIC had been hindering our mission. But once we recognized that the OIC was a micromanager, we were able to band together to maintain stability. For the rest of the workup and deployment, the whole of the platoon stayed strong and ensured the success of the platoon. Because the rest of the platoon and I were able to put unit success above the frustration the OIC caused, we were able to get into the target safely, execute our plan, and get back to our extract point without incident.

At times it may be necessary for a leader to ensure that all things are in order before an evolution. Even seasoned pilots use a checklist each and every time they fly, because they're human and can't always remember every detail of every task. Once again, the lessons-learned list becomes essential. Call it a checklist if you like, but whatever it is, it is a technique to aid you in your pursuit of success. There is no shame in referring to it, but there is much to be lost when you fail because you didn't use the resources you had to prevent problems.

There will be times when you, or someone you appoint, must ensure success by micro assessing. The tasking may be so complex that mere guidance isn't enough. Set the stage for you to be an active member of the development of the project, as a working member, and then it is less likely that your group will perceive your interaction as outside meddling.

While preparing for a job, make it known that you expect your Team to review lessons learned and to rehearse if possible. Everyone needs to realize that if they follow these simple practices, they will make fewer mistakes. Only in knowing, as completely as possible, the ways in which the Team has been successful before, how they have failed or created problems, and what their strengths and weaknesses are can you ensure the greatest possibility for success.

Navy SEALs operate at night most of the time. The veil of darkness is our friend, and we exploit it. This carries with it risks and heightens the stakes considerably. On the one hand, darkness can conceal you. On the other hand, you must negotiate unfamiliar terrain in that same obscurity. Night-vision devices are not always an option. They can ruin your natural night vision, which may become crucial. They also do not provide for peripheral vision which can be detrimental to your situational awareness. If there is not enough ambient light, such devices can be nearly useless anyway. The use of an infrared light to illuminate your target can be helpful but can also make you a beacon to anyone else using night-vision devices. So, good gear is important, but not as the end all, be all.

Each member of a platoon carries infrared strobe light and chemical sticks—break-and-shake lights like the ones kids use during Halloween, except that these are infrared. We carry other gear that can emit some useful light. There is always the flashlight in the backpack. I carry a small penlight on a lanyard around my neck, stuffed inside my shirt. This can be turned on and concealed well enough not to be obvious to others. But when seen through night-vision goggles (NVGs), these lights, small as they are, are like beacons.

Before every night evolution, and periodically throughout it, the LCPO and LPO will look at each member of the platoon with NVGs to ensure that all lights are secured. This is not micromanagement; this is ensuring safety and success.

There may have been times when you were sure micromanagement was necessary. Maybe the crew or person assigned a task just wasn't getting it, or perhaps there was someone who needed to be under scrutiny most of the time. Reflect on those instances now and reevaluate—was it necessary, or the result of a lack of initial guidance or a failing team environment? Micromanagement is dangerous and very rarely appropriate. If at times you need to spend extra time with your people, you must remember to mentor and develop, not micromanage. People will need help and additional attention, at some times more than others. But you must use these as opportunities for productive development. Learn to be a mentor rather than resorting to micromanagement.

Some people will argue that some micromanagers are innocent, that they are just doing their jobs. This situation occurs when a leader has good intentions and wants to share their knowledge but gets too involved, or knows too little and feels that constant meddling will project the illusion of knowledge and involvement. It is essential to be known among your staff as a participant, a working leader, but not at the expense of preventing your people from performing their duties. There can be a fine line between what is perceived as enthusiastic interest and overwhelming meddling. Your subordinates want to know that you care and are not aloof and beyond reproach, but at the same time they need their own realm in which to perform their duties.

CHAPTER 8 LESSONS

- Assign the job only if you trust the assignee to do it.
- Provide the necessary requirements.
- Do not hang over your workers' shoulders unless absolutely necessary.
- Do not nitpick a job well done just because it isn't a carbon copy of what you had in your mind's eye.
- Accept the results unless they are severely flawed or could cause an accident.

- Allow your Team to make and learn from mistakes, which is crucial to development.
- No matter how intuitive your Team members are, they are not mind readers. Give them the essential details, then trust their judgment and results.
- To establish a trend of second-guessing work breeds resentment. Trial and error and senior guidance are advantageous; however, do not waste time by giving someone a task without sharing all the information necessary to do the job well.
- Empowerment is the most important principle. You hired these people to do a job ... let them do it!
- If you "know it all," you just might get the chance to prove it!
- Work toward the goal. Be seen, not heard. Set the stage and let the Team go, making small steerage adjustments when necessary.
- Just because someone makes a mistake does not mean they require micromanagement. Consider whether they really had all the tools they needed to complete the job.

Chapter 9

~~❦~~

Preventive Maintenance

Time Is Money, but Support Is the Mint!

The value of maintaining your equipment should be obvious. But it is surprising how many people fail to recognize this. Every piece of equipment you use in your business has two life expectancies, one when it is maintained and another when it is not. This goes for the care and feeding of the personnel as well. Just because a problem or issue has not yet manifested itself doesn't mean it is not poised to wreak havoc on your Team.

A Navy SEAL Team operates almost exclusively in harsh environments and under extreme conditions. What SEALs perceive as ideal weather keeps everyone else indoors, and we like it that way. With these "desired" conditions comes an adverse and damaging effect on our equipment, gear, weapons, and personnel. When SEALs go into the field, all we have is what we bring with us, we only carry what we need, and it is crucial that everything work once we arrive at our objective.

Most SEAL missions, prior to 2003, originated from the water, the majority of recent operations being wholly land based. Although the

majority of today's gear is robust and well-designed for austere operations, salt water and other environmental conditions can corrode and
damage the gear if it is not properly cared for. It is imperative that we get
it across the beach or onto the objective as dry and salt free as possible.
A SEAL platoon might start a mission by jumping from a helicopter or
an airplane into the water, or swimming ashore from a boat. For a mission that requires an extended stay in a harsh climate, we must ensure
that water, whether from the ocean, a stream, or rain, does not soak the
clothing that keeps us warm and alive. Either way, we are getting wet,
dirty, and carrying sensitive equipment that must be protected. Sand,
dirt, and dust are the main concerns for most of the current operations.
That stuff seems to be able to penetrate like it was water.

To keep our gear as clean and dry as possible, we have bags made of
heavy-duty waterproof cloth or plastic with watertight zippers. A little
thing like neglecting to put grease on the zipper or allowing corrosion to
take hold can make it too noisy to be clandestine or ruin its ability to deny
water entry to the important stuff. After two hours in the water, a small
leak can soak a man's clothes (not so great in cold environments) and
render radios or other essential gear inoperable. Not maintaining a seem
ingly little thing like a zipper can compromise the success of a mission!

Although the bags are extremely durable, they can still be punctured.
The "dry bags" have nozzles on them to vent air while you compress them
to fit into your pack. To check for leaks, a man simply blows a dry bag
up and rotates it in a pan of water, the same way you'd test a bike tire for
a leak. This entire process takes about five minutes if you're being thorough. But skipping this vital check or failing to ensure the valve is closed
when you are complete with the test or compression can waste days of
planning and gear preparation, thousands of dollars of aviation fuel (if
you've been inserted by air), countless man-hours, your unit's reputation,
and possibly somebody's life, depending on what gear is ruined.

SEALs have learned these lessons over time and passed them down.
And this is why every SEAL maintains a log of lessons learned and con-

sults it regularly, to ensure that we continue to pass down good ideas and train the future. Something may seem so obvious that it can never be forgotten. It can, and at the most inopportune time. Record lessons learned and prevent catastrophe.

Leaders are vigilant. The achievement of goals is paramount, and as the leader you must be looking one step ahead of the action and encouraging you all your Team members to do the same. Preventative maintenance is applicable in that the review and maintenance of your lessons-learned log and SOPs will invariably help limit or prevent future shortfalls. Focus on the task at hand, but be aware of potential future stumbling points. You must maintain a proactive stance in order to prevent problems that could disturb the smooth and proper functioning of your Team and the flow when they're working toward common goals. This is not restricted to machinery and procedures, it includes personnel. It is a grave mistake to wait for problems to occur before dealing with them. People have emotions, concerns, interests, and families outside of the workplace. While it would be ideal if nothing personal entered the professional world, such an expectation is unrealistic. An employee with a sick family member may not show signs of distress, but they will be there, and they will affect the work that individual is able to perform for himself and for the achievement of the common objective. Do not be afraid of being human. Although there may not be anything you can do directly, a simple "How is your father doing?" could be the one nice gesture of the day that helps this person feel that he is indeed part of a Team that cares and, more importantly, that his leader is actually concerned about him and the other Team members and takes the time to ask. Be prepared to listen if they have something to say about it. Ensure your "concern" does not morph into an empty gesture. Take the time and be patient, remember what your vision is, and nurture the environment.

People are often reluctant to get too personal or are concerned that they might ask the wrong questions. They fear that they may cause offense or aggravate the problem by talking about it. Honest concern does not hurt people; isolation does. When someone has a difficult problem, the simple expression and acknowledgment that you know something is bothering him and are available to help may be enough to prevent the demoralization he might suffer if he were left to feel isolated and alone. This is not to suggest that you seek out every detail of his problem, only that you let him know that he is a part of a cohesive unit that is concerned about its members.

Handle looming issues before they become a problem, rather the ignoring it hoping it will resolve itself. Avoid this "absentee" problem-solving technique; it doesn't work in the long run. The cohesion and integrity of the Team must come first. If self-interest plagues your organization, you will not be able to foster the spirit necessary to survive. If you want to run a strong Team, this is not a rule that can be broken. There will be personality conflicts. The vigilant leader will notice these festering and deal with them before they get out of control. Your Team members don't need to like each other; they just need to know that you expect them to put their differences aside while at work and perform like professionals. If they are unable to do so, counsel them, document it, deal with it, and carry on with business.

You cannot identify a downward trend if you don't know what the trend is in the first place. How can you notice when crew members are having problems if you are engrossed with your own tasks? To be an effective leader, you will need to learn the art of dynamic interaction with people and develop a far-reaching and innovative vision. Being involved means knowing when issues arise, identifying when Team members are having problems, and expressing the fact that you are their leader and are resolute that these problems be taken care of. This might mean that you refer them to your human resources department, medical staff, or simply give them the moral support of your interest. You are and must be the custodian, and believe in it.

Never leave a man behind! This is and has been the keystone of the success of the Navy SEALs. Dead or alive, bloody or broken, everyone is coming home! It is their unwavering confidence in this fact that makes SEALs willing to go so far over the edge and into harm's way for the accomplishment of the mission. Before operations, make sure that everyone is part of the planning, the work, and the preparation of a successful mission. No one wants to put a Teammate into a risky situation unnecessarily, so every individual makes sure that he takes care of himself, his gear, and ensures that he is executing all his tasks to the best of his ability to prevent his Teammates from having to pick up the slack or worse, having to go back in to get him. Each person holds tight to their faith every member is of this mindset so if the need arises they are more than willing to go back into a risky situation to recover or assist a platoon mate. This trust and faith is a major facet of their personal and professional development as well as the achievement of the group objectives.

SEALs do everything as a Team. In competition, men seek to push, motivate, and improve their platoon mates. On liberty, in a live-fire training exercise, or in a real-world operation, the attitude is the same: The welfare and safety of the Team is of a higher priority than personal gain.

In a real-world firefight, you must win the fight before beginning your rescue efforts. It may appear that getting everyone home is not the top priority, and at that point in time it is not! The goal is and must be to win the fight. If you do not have fire superiority, rescue efforts will only produce more casualties. The fact remains, however, that come hell or high water, and whether it takes one hour, three days, or more, SEALs will get everyone home.

Your crew must arrive each day secure in the knowledge that they are going to be taken care of. They must be allowed to work without worrying about whether someone else will take credit for their labor. They must be secure in the knowledge that no one amongst the group will take advantage or purposely benefit from another another's misfortune. This trust is integral to the success and cohesion of SEALs and will be for you and your team. Trust and confidence prevents problems, from the impossibility of collaboration for fear of exploitation to isolation when dealing with personal problems.

What Makes a SEAL

Although there are no recipes for what makes a SEAL, there are two primary common factors:

Dedication to a Mission or Goal Beyond Oneself This is, in fact, a common trait among all servicemen and-women—Army, Navy, Air Force, Marines, and Coast Guard. It is the willingness to put a common goal before personal interest. The common goal is national defense. The vast majority of people who join the military are willing to work long, grueling hours for little money, to be away from home and family for months on end, and to put themselves in harm's way to defend the freedom and rights of people they do not know. A common goal and a sense of purpose, this is the power of the Team concept! The men and women of our armed forces view the country as a Team and the citizens as its members. They realize that they don't like, agree with, or even know everyone they are charged with protecting, but they perform their military duties because it is the right thing to do and in the best interest of the Country!

In the Navy SEAL Teams you will find a corps of men of the highest caliber with unwavering resolve and dedication to duty and country. This is not to say that SEALs are all from the same mold, quite the contrary. SEALs surface from a myriad of backgrounds; electrical engineers, plumbers, nurses, farmers, surfers, rich, poor, microbiologists ... the list is endless. One officer I had the honor of serving with was a Rhodes Scholar, and he would work alongside those who held only a simple high school degree. Some were reared in the hills of West Virginia and some in the most affluent settings society has to offer.

In your organization, you want and need steadfast commitment and dedication on the part of each Team member, and their refusal to quit no matter what! You must build, support, and defend a solid corps of employees, full-and part-time, and temporary, who believe in and have a vested interest in the success and achievement of the unit objective. You cannot do this as part of an isolated elitist hierarchy. If your Team sees you as an overbearing, unapproachable megalomaniac, you will merely have people working a job, not a cohesive unit of motivated personnel moving together toward a common goal. Sense the climate and adjust accordingly.

Fear of Failure and of Not Giving One's All to the Team This drives every SEAL! You know that the men with you will give every ounce of energy, and then some, for you and for the others around them. If you fail your Team, you fail yourself. When you are part of a cohesive and successful unit, the worst feeling you can have is that when you were needed, you did not come through. The opposite, of course, is the deep feeling of satisfaction for not only a job well done but also the knowledge that you and everyone else has benefited.

This is the key to any truly successful Team. You cannot force this feeling of duty and dedication on someone; it needs to come from within them. You must trust every individual, and they must trust you. Tolerance of anything less will be harmful to the overall health of your organization. Ethical issues must be handled swiftly, confidentially, and fairly.

Team Tips

Encourage Physical and Mental Fitness

A person in good physical and mental condition is less likely to get sick or miss work, and they will operate more efficiently and with more clarity and direction. They will be productive longer and will maintain a more positive self-image. Exercise gives people time to think, relieves stress, and simply gets a person's blood flowing. Those in good physical condition will be more productive during working hours. SEALs in staff positions and support personnel attached to a SEAL Team are allotted time for physical training every morning because it makes them sharper throughout the day and stronger in the long run, not to mention that top physical and mental conditioning is tied to mission success due to the nature of Special Operations. The standards are high, and so are the levels of performance and the results. This is maintenance of the body and mind and must not be overlooked. Allotting time for fitness will pay dividends; it gets your blood flowing, which provides extra oxygen to the brain stimulating clarity of thought, it gets your body warmed up, staves off stiffness, and will facilitate healthy competition.

Preventive Maintenance Is Simplicity

Little things you do now prevent large issues later. You must raise the standards of weaker Team members and never force your top performers to degrade their high standards to accommodate the less motivated. They should certainly figure out who is in need of help and mentor them, but with the expectation of bringing them up, not bringing their own standards down.

While I was in ROTC, we were required to attend P.T. three mornings per week. After the first week, several of us asked that the sessions be made more challenging. The answer came back: no. I was seeing the same environment that I had during the indoctrination course in Rhode Island which I spoke of earlier. When we inquired, the answer was that the staff was concerned that if they made the P.T. sessions too hard, the new midshipmen would become discouraged and quit. The staff had already put a cap on progress. The really motivated people would still succeed, but those with the propensity to take the easy way had just been given a rose-lined path to apathy.

After a few months the physical conditioning of the new members of the unit had not improved, and the morale of the physically fit had degraded. In this particular case, the decisions of the administration had prevented maintenance! The lack of vision and strong goals got the young midshipmen stuck in a rut. These new men believed that they were unable to achieve more, because after months of "work" they had not seen improvement. This problem took the entire next semester to fix.

Risk Assessment

Risk assessment is simply seeking out all the information about what your Team faces and determining your ability to deal with those issues. Almost every SEAL training exercise and mission is high risk. Operations may involve parachuting, rifle and pistol fire, explosives training, scuba diving, jumping from or being suspended from a helicopter, and more. While exciting, all these operations and training missions must be undertaken with the utmost professionalism, or lives will be lost.

To prevent as many mishaps as possible, SEALs use and maintain risk assessment sheets, which are filled in and scrutinized before each evolution. These sheets detail the experience level of the participants, the difficulty of the task, environmental conditions, the nature of the operation, the equipment to be used, and the physical and mental state of the participants. Other things are also listed on the sheet; these can encompass anything the men feel is pertinent to the upcoming operation or exercise. The experience and wisdom of risk assessment is geared entirely to the prevention of mishaps and accidents and the enhancement of SA through a realistic "what if" process. Strict adherence to the usage of risk assessment sheets has greatly reduced the number of training incidents within the Teams and the military. I must caution you that if you unduly burden the risk assessment process with every single contingency you will have defeated the purpose. The intent is not to limit your operations, but to enhance your awareness of possible issues so that you may be prepared to handle and mitigate them, while pressing forward towards achievement.

As SEALs, we pride ourselves on our extremely low accident rate. A risk assessment includes the completion of supervisor checks. Before any diving, shooting, demolition, or air operation, each platoon receives at least two checks from certified supervisors, who undergo a rigorous training and qualification process for their specialties. These are apart from the self and buddy checks SEALs continually perform and receive from platoon mates. We are extremely serious about our preoperational checks and never skip or deride them, because they have the potential to prevent accidents and save lives. When the jumpmaster slaps the back of your parachute and says you are good to go, you know you are. You have faith that even if you do not get along socially, as Teammates you will never allow harm to befall one another. That is the beauty of a solid and successful Team.

Keep People Dedicated to and Confident in the Team Concept

Be involved from the start, and you will not have to play catch-up later. If your Team knows you believe in the Team, they will believe in you.

Keep People Informed

Share your vision with the Team. Let them know where they are going. Let them share in your vision and enthusiasm. Providing information and insight into your plans prevents frustration and confusion.

Before I was the platoon point man, I was rear security, the last guy in the patrol, and the farthest from the plan. It could be frustrating at times to be in the back with no idea about what was going on up front. The twist being that I needed to have a heightened SA because one of the main responsibilities of rear security is that in the event contact is made in a channelized area, or one of a myriad of other situations, is responsible for becoming the point man and getting everyone out.

Lesson learned! When I became point man, I would, if the situation permitted, make my way around the platoon during stops to bring the guys up to speed on what was going on. I would tell them how far we had gone, where we were, any plan changes, and what to expect next. Not only did this make them feel more like a part of the action, but it gave them valuable, tactical information to use in a crisis, or in case the decision makers were physically incapacitated or engrossed in other issues. The feedback I got afterward was great. The simple effort it took to tell people what was going on made a huge difference to them. They were informed, aware, and satisfied.

CHAPTER 9 LESSONS

- A vigilant leader is an informed leader.
- Isolation can allow people to feel demoralized and become distant.
- Invest time in preventive maintenance now to avoid wasting time later.
- Record lessons learned to prevent catastrophes.
- Be interested in your Team members; ask them how they are doing.
- Keep people informed to prevent the frustration of "not knowing."

Chapter 10

~~◡

The Four Links

It is your responsibility as the leader and controller to ensure that the accepted perception (which is your group's reality) is consistent with the system and vision you have conceived and set in motion. Everything from innocent misinformation to malicious distortion of the facts for personal gain can affect your Team and its ability to achieve your objectives. You must keep your people informed as often and thoroughly as possible. If you have ensured everyone has the facts and the details, they will not need to look to outside sources for information or, worse, believe made-up details for a sense of fulfillment. When you keep the group abreast of current events, you diminish much of the power of the rumor network.

The concept of "close hold"—keeping your Team close-knit and self-sufficient—encompasses both the security and the sanctity of the Team as well as the ideals and environment you have chosen to foster. Build an environment that is self-sufficient, remain steadfast in the pursuit of the common vision, and stay vigilant in your protection and direction of that vision.

The word "Team suggests" that there is a common tie or thread that binds people together in the pursuit of shared goals. In times of difficulty or uncertainty, people will turn to what is familiar and comfortable. These aspects of membership, sanctity, and camaraderie must not be over-looked or undervalued. These, in fact, are advantages you must capitalize on.

We are social creatures and need interaction with and find solace in groups of people who are like-minded, who have a sense of common duty or similar goals, or whom we wish to emulate. Teams provide friendship, security, assistance, and a sense of belonging. They also meet a variety of other social and emotional needs. For some people, teams provide an extension of family; for others, it is the group or entity with which they identify, made up of people whom they simply enjoy being around and involved with.

The attitude you maintain while building, developing, and leading your Team will greatly affect you and the other members. Your Team will be what you make of it, and the easiest way to identify its needs and the needs of its members is to hone your skills of introspection and determine what qualities you expect. What is it that you look for? Are there some aspects of a group dynamic you find more desirable than others? Think about past group experiences and draw from those memories and lessons learned to improve or maintain your current situation.

We must accept that the world is a dynamic laboratory of human behavior, yet remain resolute in our determination to manipulate our environment for the good of our staff/crew and ourselves rather than let it control us. You must take ownership and be in command of what you can control, learn to leave the rest, and avoid fruitless entanglements. The true essence of leadership is the calculated, moral, and thoughtful organization of your world. Your responsibility as a leader is to mold, maintain, and develop your Team ethics, practices, and the environment in which it works.

In times of change or when the environment becomes hostile or the terrain difficult, the Team must be where your people go for support and solutions. It must be the source your people turn to for help, motivation, and inspiration. When properly maintained, it achieves a success that builds on itself. The SEALs I have had the honor of serving with cherish and look forward to showing up for work each day, even when the training schedule is grueling. Their overwhelming sense of duty, accomplishment, and belonging arises not from numbers but from safety in security.

There is consolation in the knowledge that if you have a problem, you can turn to those you surround yourself with for answers and need not worry about the information being leaked or becoming the topic of gossip. It is unrealistic to expect that no one will ever complain or be dissatisfied with their job. It is your job and duty, however, to ensure that when they do have issues, they rely on the solid, supportive Team. If there is the perception, correct or not, that they cannot count on your support, then you have failed at one of your most important tasks as a leader: the foundation and preservation of a sturdy, loyal, and available support network. If your people have concerns, you must take the time to find out what the issues really are. That is your job, your responsibility; it is a duty you assume when you accept a leadership position. You cannot use the excuse that you have no time. You have gotten to where you are due to your resume and credentials. It is expected that you have the capacity to make the time and handle difficult situations with a calculated and steady demeanor. At the very minimum, you must gain the pertinent knowledge and assign someone you trust to handle the problem.

You do not want your people looking to outside sources for support or comfort. Handle as many problems as possible internally. Your people must see the strength of the Team. If they feel that you have breached confidentiality on sensitive issues, or have treated those issues with insincerity or as trivial matters, you will lose your edge. It goes without saying that if an issue arises that does require outside help, be it medical or any other number of instances, you must be prepared to make it happen or find someone who can. In short, it is imperative that you remain open minded, for it is when they feel that you do not care that they turn elsewhere. This lack of communication can be particularly detrimental.

Deal with issues internally whenever possible. It is not appropriate to release information without the consent of the person or people involved. If you must reveal a situation you observed in your Team in order to facilitate important lessons learned or to seek the most appropriate source of resolution, you can do so, but you must make the facts clear and concise so as not to mislead or cloud the truth.

Different communities and jobs have their own jargon, which can sound foreign or confusing to outsiders. This can create grave misconceptions, which can lead to unwarranted reactions and tainted images. This perception can then become reality. Consider the young recruit calling home. He tells his mother that he had a rough day and the instructor made him "beat his face." The mother reacts in horror, imagining her bloodied son on the other end of the telephone. Because she doesn't know that "beat your face" simply means to do push-ups, she now has a distorted and negative view of the instructor, and the military!

The possibilities for miscommunication increase when dealing with issues of greater magnitude. Study language to become a more effective communicator. Identifying the nuances of language used in different communities, organizations, companies, and groups brings to light the rapidity with which the intention and meaning of oral communication can be misconstrued. When talking to those outside of your Team, make sure you explain the details in standard English to avoid the misconception or misinterpretation of jargon.

Linking Principles:

Comfort in solace!
Solace in trust!
Trust in security!
Security in the Team!

Linking principles of cohesion is fundamental and crucial to the survival of a Team. If any of these are breached or tainted, you have squandered a portion of a link or an entire one, which may lead to the compromise of unit integrity. Over the past decade the collapse of several major corporations and a host of midsized and small companies resulted from this chain being broken. We have also witnessed the heads of several of these large groups highlighted for their unscrupulous conduct. Their self-absorption ruined the lives of many customers and employees. Those who held the leadership roles violated and exploited the trust their Teammates had in them. They left people behind—their own employees, their investors, those who held their companies' stocks in 401Ks and other retirement accounts, and, in some instances, the American taxpayer. At some point these people abandoned the dedication and pursuit of the common good they offered and focused on personal gain.

If, in a leadership position, you plan to deceive your Team, you willfully sacrifice your honor. They look to their leader for wisdom and guidance, and they trust that a leader will take care of them. The maligned, self-righteous leader is a treacherous entity and has no place on a Team. The mere presence of such an individual destroys all that they might have achieved by their personal vision. Hold the four links in high regard and maintain them, preventive action being the most advantageous. Remain in tune with the condition of the links and keep them strong.

Comfort in solace: This stems from the level of comfort that one finds when they know that their partners sustain the same reverence for the fundamental operation and framework of the Team. People seek membership in those groups with which they can identify. It follows that if they are secure in the knowledge that they are among likeminded people or people who hold similar goals and ambitions dear, they will experience a greater sense of comfort.

Solace in trust: Once you have identified the group that reveres the same ideals and practices, you will form a bond. The notion of sanctity in trust is an internal ethic. Personal standards must be genuine in each member. One person who lacks resolve can destroy the natural strength of an experienced Team and decimate a fledgling one. Those who would violate the trust of another must not be allowed to remain on the Team.

Trust in security: With likeminded people who sustain the veneration of trust, you, as the leader, must ensure that the security they now feel is not debased. The Team has developed through the first two steps naturally. As the leader, you are ever mindful of situations or issues that could potentially discredit the secure boundaries of your Team. You cannot detach yourself and become aloof. In accepting the leadership role, you relinquished the luxury of deniability. You cannot say, "Well, it wasn't my responsibility," because when you're the person in charge, everything is! If a junior person screws up, you had better believe that the eyes of scrutiny will be cast upon the senior member. That's just the way it is. This is a fact of leadership and a burden you must be willing to bear. The overall security and integrity is in your hands, and you must protect it.

Security in the Team: The recognition of like ideals is coupled with a belief in trust. You are the omnipresent provider of security and integrity! After your Team has established the first three links, the entire group will move into the final stage: security. You are now at the point where the likeminded people have gelled as a group and have identified the fact that you, their leader, are the bastion of Team integrity. But in a subtle and sure movement from personality-based leadership to Team-oriented duty and responsibility, Team members now look for support within the organization. They will bring you that new and great idea and look to you to choose, evaluate, improve, and implement good ideas. They will count on you to maintain close hold of that information. When they have personal problems, they know they can count on the Team to do everything within reason to lessen the severity of their misfortune. They know that you are there because you believe in them and that you will not throw them under the bus for personal gain.

Preventing a Break in the Links

Rumor and Gossip

You cannot tolerate malicious rumor or gossip, and you certainly can't participate yourself. People will talk about other people ... that is human nature. It is not your job to weasel around the break room sniffing out every little story. That is neither effective nor appropriate.

Your best approach to stifling destructive rumors is to prevent them in the first place. Fostering a strong atmosphere and providing timely information are your most effective tools. When people feel left behind or in the dark, they start to talk. Their natural curiosity or need to know will surface. Since they are not getting information from the leader, they will try to solve the mystery of lack of information among themselves. Theories will filter through the workplace, and soon it will be hard for people to tell truth from fiction.

Not all information is suitable for mass consumption. You must use your discretion and experience when determining what information needs to be disseminated. There will be times, and they are difficult to discern, when information is not fully developed enough to release. Generating a revolving rumor mill can be devastating to the smooth ebb and flow of information. Depending on the size of your group, the rumors can be very difficult to cull once set free. When there is vital information that affects the Team, however, you must inform all concerned as soon as possible, allowing enough time for them to react appropriately, whenever you are able to.

See that every situation is handled at the lowest possible level. There are certain situations that not everybody needs to know about. Inform your Team about the type of situations you want to be notified of. You don't need to know that Joe is out of printer ink, but you do need to know if he was just in an automobile accident. When I was new to the Teams, I was determined to do everything right. I attacked every task with a zealous fervor and reported to my chief promptly upon completion. After a few months he stopped me, saying that he really didn't need to hear every detail of every second of every day because he had a lot of things to do besides listen to me report. I said, "Roger that, Chief. What do you want to know?" He looked at me with a grin and replied, "As long as I'm not gonna get shotgunned on the carpet in front of the skipper, I don't need to know about it."

He wanted to know about issues that might concern people by virtue of their severity. Getting "shotgunned" means having someone grill you about something you should know about but don't. "On the carpet" means standing in front of the commanding officer in his office . . . usually with the door shut. "Skipper" is just another term to refer to the commanding officer. If Chief wasn't going to have to deal with it, he didn't need to know about it.

What does and doesn't, and what should or shouldn't, get reported is unique to each organization. The amount of information required by the leadership is often a function of time, the situations at hand, and the decisions to be made. Planning long-range strategy demands a different type and amount of information than making sure an angry customer gets satisfaction. Give your working leaders the tools to exercise information triage and weed out what you don't need to or want to know about. You will need to set the stage for your Team and explain what you expect from them. Make it part of your SOP!

Malicious or Inadvertent Spreading of Sensitive Information

If all events of the day become immediate public knowledge, there can be serious fallout. This is especially important when dealing with counseling and personal issues. Confidentiality concerning evaluations is paramount. If you counseled an individual about a potentially damaging issue and promised to keep it confidential, it must remain just that. You cannot use it against them later, ever. If you are unable to make that commitment, do not make the guarantee.

Before you talk to someone about sensitive information, determine their need to know. Make sure that everyone understands this principle. Unscrupulous individuals sometimes utilize others' deeply personal or private information for their own gain. These people, who violate the Team's trust in order to improve their own status, are a thorn in the side of any organization and must not be tolerated. Let it be known that abuse of the privacy policy has severe consequences. What the result will be is too unique to each unit for me to offer a reasonable standard.

We have already discussed the vast importance of security. In addition to the controlled release of information, you must consider the leadership's capacity to deal with specific issues. A minor infraction taken straight to the top may lead to a perception that the offense is of a greater magnitude than it really is. Furthermore, the leader is faced with the prospect of solving the problem. The choices are to send it back down the chain of command or deal with it. It is important that if issues arrive at your desk without having gone through the proper chain of command, you send them back to the beginning. If you allow people to skip their leadership, you set your Team up for failure.

Stress the necessity of handling issues at the lowest level. This ensures that all concerned are informed, and it relieves you from having to deal with the small day-to-day happenings. A breach of the chain of command sends damaging signals that the Team lacks structure which will eventually undermine your ability to control. People need and desire structure, the lack of which can ruin a great Team or prevent it from developing.

Make the need for discretion and confidentiality perfectly clear to the Team leadership and every member of the Team. How you handle sensitive information will affect the lives of your people, the development of your subordinates, and the success of your Team. You cannot treat serious, personal matters as a joke or allow them to become the subject of gossip. You cannot tolerate such behavior from your Team.

The security your Team provides its members is the greatest asset you have in any organization. To neglect the maintenance of that comfort or to allow it to be subverted by rumors and deceit is the mark of bad, irresponsible leadership. When I was a boy and had done something wrong, my father would sit me down before doling out my punishment. He would explain my infraction and suggest that in the future, before I acted upon my boyish instincts, I should apply the "reasonableman test": If you are doing something, or about to, and it does not feel right, stop and think. If it seems wrong to release information, it probably is. When in doubt, there is no doubt. The exploitation of information for personal gain is wrong! Be proactive and vigilant in your role as a leader. This is your Team, and it is your responsibility to protect it.

I offer another experience to highlight the advantages and aweinspiring achievements of a well-oiled and structured Team environment. My first assignment was to SEAL Delivery Vehicle Team Two (SDVT-2) in Virginia. Those assigned to SDVs must undergo several months of additional training to earn qualifications to operate advanced dive equipment and the SDV. It is a battery operated mini-sub less than 30 feet long. It is a wet sub, which means the occupants are exposed to the ambient environment during operations. We do have some underwater communications equipment, but the majority of the operation is completed using hand signals and well-rehearsed timing. SDV operations are some of the most challenging and delicate operations. There are many moving parts and people involved. A break in the organization of the flow and establishedstandards can rapidly turn a high risk evolution into a salvage operation. The standard deployment of an SDV is from the dry deck shelter mounted to the back of a U.S. Navy submarine. This makes the complexity of SDV operations grow exponentially now that you are intertwining two very successful, established, but different groups, and finding ways to mesh tactics and SOPs. It is absolutely imperative that these two groups conduct business with clear communication and an established avenue to the end state. The safety of the entire submarine, its crew, and the SEALs involved all hinge on a seamless flow of communication, trust, and the ability to conceive rapid solutions in the event the normal flow is derailed.

The SDV is launched and recovered while the submarine remains submerged. In order for it to remain submerged and controlled it must be underway. So, now you are looking at launching an SDV and recovering it while the sub is underway, its large screw (prop) churning just aft of the launch and recovery site. There are several men working outside of the sub during this period, setting up and breaking down the rigging required for the operations. Accountability and trust in your platoon mates is absolutely essential. Trust in the submarine crew is paramount. Your SA must remain sharp. Submerged in the complete and utter darkness of the ocean, the undersea world flowing by, pulling on you as you work to set the rigging and not be ripped away. The force of the passing water is too rapid to swim back into position if you lose your bearing. Hand signals and the flow gained in rehearsals guide your every movement.

If you are pulled away, will your platoon notice or will you be swept into the churning screw before you can make it to the surface? Even if they do notice, the train is moving and it will take a great deal of time to redirect efforts to the recovery of personnel, which is wholly dependent on the priority of the mission. They will come back, they will find me, and I will not be left behind—that is for sure. You have that faith and would never doubt it for a second because you know that if the tables were turned you would exhaust all avenues to recover a buddy. This WILL happen, but after the set and required objectives are met. The operation must be executed, the goal must be met, the commander's intent fulfilled, and the mission accomplished first.

That is the only way you can plan and execute high risk missions or complete complex taskings. The Team knows they are solid; they have faith in their comrades and know beyond a shadow of a doubt that if trouble arises the objective will be met and all members will be taken care of. Keep in mind that this is merely the launch and recovery process; now add the hazards inherent to the missions. Still, the group stays strong when they are driven by the pursuit and achievement of the common goal.

Chapter 10 Lessons

- Close hold is about confidentiality as well as the maintenance of the ideals and foundation of the Team.
- A degraded or missing fundamental link defiles the Team and will prevent it from operating as a Team.
- Teams are based on comfort in security, not safety in numbers.
- Control damaging rumors by keeping your Team and those concerned informed in a timely manner.
- Support your Team's chain of command and let it work by backing your leadership and their decisions.
- When in a quandary about what to do or who needs to know what, apply the "reasonable person test."
- Do not lose control of your Team through the inappropriate dissemination of information.

Chapter 11

~~~

Teammates, Not Lackeys

Even the best-trained and most highly motivated people require structure. Any group of men and women working together, regardless of their experience, will still need a chain of command. That chain must be strong and provide the rest of the Team with the comfort of knowing that their leadership and support structures will work and be there for them. Leeway for the individual to act, to be empowered to make decisions and critical changes while working to achieve goals, is not only necessary but beneficial to the growth of both the individual and the Team. But too much latitude can be detrimental. If you have a mixed group of new and experienced Team members, those with more training and know-how must set the example at all times. If they don't, your new Teammates may not have the mental, physical, or emotional resources and direction to draw upon when faced with important tasks. But this training by example will also be important when the new people later become the mentors for the Team.

The men of the Naval Special Warfare community are unique among the military ranks for several reasons. U.S. Navy SEALs, officers and enlisted men alike, go through the same training, side by side. There is no difference between the training officers and enlisted men receive. From this a common tie is drawn. It is much easier for a SEAL officer to relate to and understand what his men are going through because he has done or is doing the same thing. Officers are afforded certain accoutrements, privileges, and extra work in conjunction with their rank, yet they are aware of what their men experience and are conscious of the ramifications of their decisions. The relationship between SEAL officers and enlisted personnel soon becomes one of mutual understanding, support, and complementary actions. Officers do not exploit their men, and the men watch out for and take care of their officers. The officers treat the men with the utmost respect and demand extra effort from them, and in turn get the very best from the men.

Anyone who strays from this code of conduct will soon find himself drummed out of the corps for not being a Team player. This includes men who act selfishly, who strive to achieve their own goals rather than the Team's, and who are micromanagers, complainers, or destructive gossips. Every man must carry his own weight, as well as the weight of every member of the Team, at all times. No Team member is ever left behind.

Before I executed my orders to BUD/S, I worked for an officer in the regular Navy who took glee in wallowing in what he perceived to be his own greatness. While working for this man, I wasted countless hours performing tasks required mostly because of his own ego. Tedious busy-work filled every gap in each already packed workday. He was outwardly arrogant and unwilling to admit when he was in error. It was obvious that everything he did was geared toward making himself look better. He would often claim others' successes as his own. And when he thought there was even a chance that something would make him look bad, without hesitation he would point a finger at someone else. He would do or say anything to make someone else take the burden for his shortfalls. His own arrogance allowed him to believe that he was loved by all. His actions were so transparent you almost felt bad for the guy because he was obviously living in a world of delusion. The sailors I worked with who had good ideas ended up remaining silent because they knew he would just claim the ideas for his own and they would receive nothing for their additional effort or loyalty.

Even worse, the men and women in his command had pressing personal issues that needed attention; and on countless occasions, his subordinates (including me) would fill in the proper paperwork for personal requests and forward them through the proper channels, only to have him deny them outright. He denied my first five requests to attend BUD/S. He said it would reflect poorly on his retention numbers.

People like this may enjoy the temporary outward appearance of success, at least in the eyes of their superiors. But this kind of selfishness always catches up to them. This officer wound up with the lowest reenlistment record for his personnel among his fellow officers. He had rocketed up the chain of command, only to lose the confidence of his men and women, and then his chance for command and retention.

This is an example of why it is crucial that you take charge of your organization and mold it into a hotbed of motivation, creativity, and ideas. The way you develop and support your group dynamic will have a profound effect on the junior and advancing personnel in your organization and will influence both the longevity and the quality of your Team. This, in turn, will directly affect the tasks they have to do and the goals they have to achieve in the years to come. This is all to support those who work with you.

You should not do away with the rites of passage or remove the duties of the junior personnel. To do so could adversely affect morale. There must be a natural maturation process. You must properly indoctrinate junior members into the Team. If they are privy to your high standards and are part of the Team's success up front, they will be more motivated and dedicated to their own development.

The goal of leadership is to provide an atmosphere where Team members motivate themselves and govern their actions for the good and well-being of the whole. People who get treated by you or other Team members as lackeys will feel they have little importance in the long run. Teammates are assets to be developed and supported; ideally, they will be productive and satisfied members of a winning and successful organization. Teammates will support and protect you, whereas lackeys will let you fall!

At my second SEAL Team I was entrusted with the duty of running the training cell's land warfare department. I was the senior enlisted person in the chain of command concerning land warfare tactics development and scheduling and training of the platoons preparing to deploy. I was still new to high-profile leadership positions and was determined not to treat any member of my Team as a lackey or a gofer. I consulted my lessons-learned book and combed it for the leadership glitches of others I had witnessed in my time in the Navy. One of my highlighted notes was about servile labor without adequate information about purpose or goal. I promised myself that my men would be informed, efficiently worked, well trained, and encouraged to become self-motivated. I pored over training schedules, made revisions, and assigned people tasks that fit their expertise. I took on my share of the work as a functioning member of my Team.

Almost all of the men working for me in my training cell had more experience than I did, and I was in charge by virtue of my rank. Other elements highlighted in my lessons-learned log dealt with effective leadership skills I had seen in my time in the Navy. Leaders who'd gotten their hands dirty with the other men in order to foster unity and to pass on valuable knowledge had set a powerful example. Leaders I'd admired were already present in the morning when we showed up, and they were still there when the men went home for the day. I wanted to be that kind of leader.

But in my efforts to be the "super leader" I neglected to consider the mountain of paperwork and other duties associated with my new position. And I still had training to complete in order to be effective at my job. In short, I had not yet made the full transition from worker to leader. I had taken on too much.

At the same time, we were understaffed and I was determined not to overwork my men. After a couple months of my whirlwind schedule, my staff approached me. They asked if we could all sit down and talk. I was exhausted and in need of sleep, but I always made time for my men, so the six of us sat down together. They said they felt I was taking on too much work and not giving them enough. I realized then that I had been obsessed and overzealous in my pursuit of developing a strong and satisfied Team and was failing to efficiently delegate and empower.

One of the guys looked at me and said, "Hey, you need to concentrate on your job and delegate more tasks to us, we're getting too much sleep." We all laughed, but I got the point. We talked for the next hour, and I started doling out new assignments. It was a great feeling to have my men care that much for their jobs, the success of the mission, and me, and I was pleased that they'd taken the time to talk to me about it. I was also glad that I had worked for great leaders who had always taken the time to listen to me, so that I had learned to grant my men the same right. Later that evening when I was in bed, getting ready to drift off to sleep, I reflected on the day. I was elated at the performance of my Team. It was then that the true spirit and effectiveness of a great Team became evident. I had gone overboard to ensure that they were happy and taken care of, so when it became apparent that I was overworking myself, they'd come to me to resolve the issue. It had been obvious to them that my interest was in their well-being and the success of our mission: the training of war fighting platoons. Had I not been an ardent proponent of the Team experience, they would have most likely let me work myself into failure. They had not. I'd made mistakes with good intentions, wanting only the betterment of the Team. And my Team had taken care of me.

That is the beauty of a solidly founded and cooperative organization. The members of your Team are the future. You cannot treat your Teammates like lackeys or you will have transcended the boundaries of leadership and slipped back into the role of a manager. Members of a highly effective and successful Team cooperate among themselves and share a common purpose. Avoid throwing your Team into jobs without explaining the connection to the completion of goals. You cannot afford to have your Team undertake seemingly fruitless labor. Inform them when you can, and they will understand when you cannot.

In your organization you are sure to have young people fresh out of college bristling with idealism and knowledge. That is a wonderful and necessary asset, but it does not replace or compare to the knowledge and practice of experienced employees. A college degree is indicative of trainability, well-roundedness, and a thirst for knowledge. These qualities combined with the real-world experience of loyal employees can be powerful tools, not only for the achievement of Team goals but for your professional development and that of your Team members. Entrust the core of experienced employees with managing the fundamental operation of the workforce. Let the new members infuse the work environment with enthusiasm, energy, and excitement about the tasks at hand, and encourage them to provide new perspectives on routine tasks. Your job is to train future leaders, not to wring the life out of subordinates. How you handle them will be how they handle their subordinates in the future.

You must be visible, interested, and vigilant. Your vision, and that of your Team, will include the outlook and mission of your organization. Share with your Team the big picture and the experience of longevity. Make it obvious that they are not toiling for a paycheck; rather, they are producing a foundation upon which the vision of the Team will stand. Mutual respect is not merely a good idea, it is necessary if you and your Team are to succeed.

CHAPTER 11 LESSONS

- The goal of a Team is to develop its members, not work them into submission.

- Involve the Team in the attainment of goals by keeping them informed.
- If you respect and support your Team, they will revere and protect you.
- Mutual respect is paramount.

Chapter 12

What Is Expected from You

Survival in today's business world demands a shift from the old paradigm of managerial "leadership" to that of true leadership. It is no longer enough to run a tight ship by the books and merely do what is expected of you. You need to be out front, leading your Team to victory by direction and example. They will expect their leader to set goals and standards, see that they are met, and follow through with decisions affecting the group. Your Team members need you to fill that role and perform well. When you provide your staff with the solid leader they demand, you are doing your job. You have the latitude to adapt, change, revamp, and customize your style. Your options are limitless (within reason) and afford you the opportunity to effect real change in your organization and its future.

Until now, everything in this book has been geared toward helping you learn to control your environment, develop your Team, and maintain it. Now is the time to think about what your comrades or employees need and expect from you. One does not become a great leader by virtue of time spent in the trenches; it requires learningfrom the experience.

Having been a member of the workforce prior to coming into a leadership position is by no means a guarantee of success. The information and experiences you have gained can only be as useful and beneficial as your application of the lessons learned to your present situation and your long-term goals. If you choose to ignore vital lessons learned, you choose to fail.

Reflect for a moment on the leaders you have known in your past. Write down their names; next to each name, identify that person as a good or a bad leader. Now annotate the list further: Were they poor or exceptional? Identify the qualities, or lack thereof, that made them so, in your opinion. Ask yourself what you needed in a leader at that time in your life. What do you need now? I encourage you to use these notes to draw up a quick matrix. Reflect on all the details you can remember to obtain a fair assessment of each person.

Now that you have refreshed your notion of the qualities of good and bad leaders, I am willing to bet that some of the traits you found in your exceptional leaders were confidence, knowledge, and honesty. On the bad side, you might have listed arrogance, lack of vision, poor communication skills, and narrow-mindedness. Apply these standards to yourself, assessing your own leadership. Does your self-evaluation match your Team's perception of you?

While you can't know exactly what others think of you, you can, through this self-evaluation, determine what you think of your leadership skills and what kind of leader you think you are. But be careful. You might ask, "What is expected of me?" and answer, "I am in charge! I'm the one who should be doing all the expecting!" This self-righteous and elitist attitude will increase the risk of alienatingyour people. If you have acted or managed this way in the past, you may find that an ineffective and divisive "us against them" attitude exists in your workplace. If your Team members have the perception that they cannot trust you, they will not be willing to go that extra mile when you need it the most. Begin today to rectify the situation by acting and leading in a way that says that the Team—which encompasses the well-being and professional development of its members, including you—is the most important aspect of your workplace. Your Team members will work for you. But you must fulfill your responsibility. The coach may be the one calling the shots, but he or she is nonetheless part of that group.

You must let your Team know that you will be there, in one way or another, if they truly need help. In all matters, personal and professional, your crew must feel that they can count on one another. For example, if there is a death in someone's family, that person must know that you will make every reasonable effort to give them time to take care of family matters. The rest of the Team must want to pick up the slack, knowing that if they were in the same situation, the others would do the same thing for them. If you advocate and promote a strong Team atmosphere, it will begin to build on itself. Your Team members will see that you have their interests in mind, and you will find that when you need help, the crew or staff is there for you. The results you will get from a Team wanting to help will be tenfold over those of a group of people begrudgingly meeting a deadline.

It is important to develop and maintain an experienced group, or training cell, for the purpose of instructing and preparing new Team members. Every Team has its own idiosyncrasies, regardless of the tasks and goals involved, and it is much more efficient to teach new people how a Team works than to wait for them to learn on their own. You need to inform new arrivals of everything you can to get them started on a solid footing, and then you must watch to make sure they are able to ask questions and feel comfortable doing so.

Your training cell will consist of trusted individuals who have proven to be effective and productive role models and mentors. Effectiveness goes much further than just high productivity; an effective training-cell leader brings the entire package. A person can be highly productive at their job yet lack the leadership traits necessary to develop and train people. This is of critical importance. When you establish a proper training cell, it forms the vital first impressions a new member gets of the Team, and it will frequently set the stage for that new member's development. The members of the training cell should be the people who have the best mix of intelligence, knowledge of the Team and its goals, and ability to form solid interpersonal relationships. Having this established training crew provides for continuity and also helps the re-invention of the wheel with the utilization of lessons learned. Your investment in your new Team-mates will become your profit, and the Team's, in the future. When your Team members perceive that the person in charge of their livelihood is strong-willed and confident, it puts the entire organization at ease. The security you provide allows everyone to concentrate on their jobs instead of wondering how they will put food on the table or whether you will support their needs as they work towards common goals. Lack of confidence in a leader is disconcerting. A milquetoast and passive demeanor inspires nothing but doubt about whether the leader is able to stand up when difficult issues arise.

It is not required that a leader be expert in every aspect of every job within the organization. It is imperative, however, that you have a thorough enough working knowledge to be able to communicate intelligently and productively, both in the conduct of day to day business and for crisis management. If you come to them to solve a problem and cannot even speak about the issue, you're beginning with a deficit. The more you educate yourself, the more confident you will be around them. You will feel more in tune with them and better able to communicate. This is inspiring to them and crucial to your success.

You must pursue and acquire knowledge continuously, both about the inner workings of your unit, their jobs, and their personal needs, and about the environment in which you compete. Go to your people to learn. Often, they will know more about the competitive environment than you do, because they are on the front lines all the time. They expect you to use them for their wealth of knowledge, and when you do, it will do much for their morale.

Moreover, your personnel want to be challenged. If they are not, they will grow bored and listless. They will lose sight of the importance of the goals you have set and will perform their tasks competently but without enthusiasm, without wanting or feeling the need to excel. Your self-assurance must translate into confidence in your Team members, as a group and as individuals. You must have the confidence to let them take risks and allow them to break out. Sometimes they will succeed immediately; other times they will need to try and fail in order to eventually achieve success. As long as the result of this is the betterment of the individual and the Team, it is permissible and will move you toward your goals.

Members of a properly developed Team will invite challenge. They will look to you to encourage an environment of innovative and creative thinking. They will want to perform new tasks, regardless of the difficulty. They will learn everything they can, from internal and external resources to affect their success in the common goals.

At no time must one Team member perceive that they continually work harder while receiving less than another; or that others are getting something for nothing. It is more important that the individual Team member pay attention to what they are doing and accomplishing rather than what they think the man or woman next to them is doing or getting. As in all things, you can facilitate this by being as open and free with information about efforts, goals, and achievements as possible.

Be straightforward and honest but tactful. Do not insult or demean people. The group needs you to be consistent and faithful to them and to the truth. They need to know that you truly mean what you say. If you need to admonish a member for any reason, make a reasonable effort to do it in private so they don't feel eviscerated in front of their peers. Euphemisms and passive language confuse and unseat your Team. Its leader must be stable and able to communicate without equivocation.

Preventive maintenance is the essence of simplicity. Little things you do now prevent large issues later. Raise the standards of the weaker members, and never force your hot runners to compromise their high standards to accommodate less motivated Team members.

As I mentioned before, while in ROTC I was required, along with the rest of the unit, to attend physical training sessions three mornings per week. The sessions weren't challenging, and we requested tougher workouts. But the administration feared that this would turn some recruits away.

The members of the ROTC unit needed the senior members to be aggressive achievers and to challenge them. They needed motivation and incentive to do better during physical training. The instructors failed the class as a whole when they tried to achieve a short-term goal by coddling the weaker people. The administrators may have thought they were helping, but they perpetuated the weaker people's weaknesses.

The following semester I was placed in charge of physical training, and I fixed the problem. I offered the better conditioned members a challenging regimen of exercise and encouraged the weaker folks to do as many perfectly performed exercises as possible rather than the required number. It was more important that they do some repetitions perfectly than all of them poorly. This provided the maximum good for all concerned. The better conditioned members had attainable goals to work for in the short term. The weaker, less physically-conditioned people were able to see what they would eventually achieve. We all worked together. Everyone felt challenged and had great workouts without getting injured. The other members of the unit were able to concentrate on exercise because it was obvious to them that I had the knowledge to train them wisely. Before every new exercise I explained the correct way to execute it without causing injury. This way they got stronger with less pain, and understood the goal was to make them better, not just to harass them.

As I mentioned before, a complaining sailor is a happy sailor, and if he's not complaining, something is wrong. Think of it this way: If those working for you quietly and passively do their work, that is what you will get—quiet and passive action. On the other hand, consider the benefits of a workforce not content with the norm and always open to and looking for a better way.

Avoid becoming obsessed with reinventing the wheel, but have the willingness to explore and develop ideas. Do not be afraid of change. What you may consider complaining could just be someone expressing a new, and quite possibly better, way of getting the job done. On the other hand, you need to quell unproductive bickering immediately. The entire Team will count on you (or the person you've assigned for this) to extinguish detrimental conflict in a timely and professional manner. Handle all disputes on the scene if possible. Leaving conflicts unaddressed tends to inflame opinion or diminish the lesson. If you enter into or notice a potentially or developed "hot" situation, determine whether it is appropriate to allow a cooling-off period. If your subordinate asks for a little time away from a situation, it is probably advisable to allow it. Let cooler heads prevail and mitigate unnecessary conflict.

You may find that some of your people will have put in more time in the workforce than you, depending on the type of work you do and your position within the organization. It is natural to feel slightly unworthy when put in charge of and tasked with leading those who have more experience. Training war-fighting platoons put me over men with more time in the Navy and of higher ranks than me. But I suppressed my doubting impulses and took the reins, thinking of the success of all involved. They didn't need a leader who was afraid of them; they needed one who held the goals and betterment of the platoon and its members in the highest regard.

When you assume a leadership position, remember that someone chose you for the position and gave you the responsibility because they believed you could do it. Your responsibility is to step up to the challenge and take control of your environment, even when this is exceptionally difficult. Assess your situation and formulate your leadership plan. Create a strong vision and mission statement, and with these, set the stage. Act effectively and with conviction. This is expected from you.

If you fail to take charge, your Team will not have confidence in you, and someone else will. Lead from the front with conviction and your Team will succeed.

CHAPTER 12 LESSONS

- Your Team requires that you:
1. Have confidence in your ability to lead.
2. Know enough about your organization to be able to speak about any potential issue. If something new arises, educate yourself immediately and handle it.
3. Be honest and forthright. Do not pull punches with your Team. They need you to be truthful and to the point.
- Experience is a part of, but not the only ingredient to, Team success. The Team needs your open-mindedness, confidence in their abilities, and respect. They need you to set strong goals and allow them the freedom to achieve those goals.

Conclusion

Lessons Learned

A Navy SEAL instructor gave the order "Forward march" through a bullhorn. Then he bellowed, "Everybody wants to be a Frogman on a sunny day!"

My entire BUD/S class linked arms and walked toward the crashing waves with apprehension. It was one o'clock in the morning, and we were already soaked and chilled to the bone. Those of us still shivering were the lucky ones. The ones who had transcended the boundary into hypothermia and exhaustion plodded forward in a near-catatonic state, too cold and battered to shiver any longer.

Ocean water splashed around my boots, then higher. The cold that came with it cut through my clothes, biting, slicing my skin like razor blades. We continued to shuffle forward until the water was knee-deep. "Halt!" bellowed the instructor through the bullhorn. "Taaaaaake seats!" The class collapsed into the water, arms solidly linked.

This had been our fifth trip to the surf zone that night; we were entering our fourth hour of sitting in the water. The instructors "requested" that we sing the theme song to Gilligan's Island, again! The words spilled out of our mouths as the waves contorted the line of men. Fatigued men whipped about like an intoxicated serpent in the pounding surf. Our arms ached with fatigue as we battled to keep them linked with those of the men next to us. If the chain broke, we'd earn more time in the water.

Our class leader, a former Marine Corps officer, yelled words of motivation and encouragement through numb, blue lips. To break our spirit, the instructors and their staff dissuaded this behavior, yet they privately admired his tenacity and leadership ethic.

Rip currents pulled the center of the class, and breakers pounded the ends, tearing at our ranks. The waves frequently interrupted my gaze, fixed as it was on the dark, featureless horizon. Immediately prior to impact, a mixed concert of mumblings warned of an incoming barrage of water. Hundreds of pounds of water smashed the class to the sandy bottom. Sandy water swirled around our heads, filling every orifice with salty grit.

The wave passed, and we collected ourselves to sit upright, arms still linked. Our abdominal muscles ached with tension as we fought to stay upright, closer to the precious oxygen provided by the salty ocean breeze.

Thirty minutes later, the lead instructor gave the orders that freed us from the icy, roaring ocean. He gathered the class in front of him, our arms still linked. "Everybody wants to be a Frogman on a sunny day," he said again. He and his men had wanted a quitter, but they didn't get one. The class and our Team spirit triumphed that night.

To some this may seem harsh treatment for any indoctrination or rite of passage. But "surf torture" is designed to test the will of prospective SEALs. The special operations profession is a game of high stakes in which men cannot afford to have companions who won't remain when the conditions are dire. We had all volunteered to be there, and we could all volunteer to leave. Every bit of training we received as prospective

SEALs, we had chosen. We didn't get to pick what happened next, but we did choose to be there to take it. We endured as a matter of choice.

Everybody wants to be in charge on a sunny day! Leadership is not bathing in the glory of your Team's effort. It is not reaping the spoils of a great day on the job. Leadership is accepting appropriate levels of risk and enduring the hard and trying times. As a leader, you must relish the tough times. You must take control of adversity and turn it into circumstances you and your Team can live and succeed with.

The position of a leader requires the responsibilities associated with being a mentor and role model. You will get calls late at night. You will have to return early from a family function to handle a blossoming problem. You must be a leader for the duration and in every instance, because consistency is paramount to your credibility and the efficient functioning of your Team. Your fortitude and stoicism will carry you through the tough times. Your example and commitment will be the life ring your people cling to in times of strife.

Moreover, the leadership role is voluntary. You may need a job and an income, but your decision to be a leader rather than a follower was strictly your choice. When you sought and accepted the position, whether consciously or not, you recognized the added and daunting responsibilities associated with it.

Leadership is a journey, not a goal or destination! Rely on the basics and a strong foundation. The principles of repetition of duties and recording lessons learned will be integral to your success. Find a point in any exercise or function to which Team members can return for a fresh start, a check point or "systems check." If step three becomes a stumbling point, return to step two. Don't be afraid to repeat work or thought processes if it will help you toward your Team and individual goals.

Leadership is about effecting change for the betterment of your organization. Provide your vision and realistic and attainable goals and guide its members in their pursuit of success. Remember, your responsibility as a leader goes beyond the simple meeting of standards. You must challenge and motivate your Team. You must provide the mentorship and professional development to help them achieve a greater level of accomplishment and fulfillment.

If you treat your Team members with respect and remain cognizant of their needs, they will become a satisfied and fulfilled entity. Take the time to find out who is working for you. Though you will periodically have to ask individual members to sacrifice for the common goal, always remember that each member is human and has individual needs—career, personal, and otherwise—that must be met for them to be an effective part of your organization.

Take the time and energy to discover strengths and weaknesses in each of your people and to utilize each individual where they will be happy and most effective. Your Teammates will be more dedicated and innovative when they are dealing with familiar and appealing material. You must use your personnel wisely. Do not waste your Team's time and effort on frivolous tasks. Busywork is not ever appropriate. If you assign someone tasks, even as extra instruction, make sure it has a useful outcome.

Your Team must know where you are coming from. Leadership is not a game, and people are not mind readers. Make your goals, rules, and expectations clear. Share your vision and explain how you plan to achieve it. In your construction and implementation of that vision, keep your self-image in perspective. Understand that you are in charge, but temper your actions with the realization that though you are the leader, you are still a member of the Team.

Keep a logbook or computer file with all your notes and lessons learned, and share them! When you encounter a familiar problem, you can avoid reliving tragedy as you attempt to solve it. I am sure you will think that you'll remember all the lessons, just as I assured myself I could. But you should keep the file handy and leave your memory and brainpower available for more important tasks!

Fortune is to be shared. Success is empty if it is not a joint reward. In the SEALs, when someone figures out a new and better way, you share it.

When you are promoted and start receiving a bigger paycheck, you take your platoon out for a treat. This is a long-standing Navy tradition we call a "wetting down." You can always find a flyer advertising free beer courtesy of a newly paid or promoted SEAL. It is a way to say, "I am successful because of you guys, for if not for the efforts of all, I would not be enjoying these accoutrements!"

The wonderful aspect of leadership is that your style, vision, goal, and situation are yours to mold. Stick to the basics and flavor your style with your life experiences. If you expect hard work from your Team, you must exemplify the sterling work ethic to be emulated. Never be satisfied with your current model. You must continually develop your leadership tactics.

The path of the true Team leader is arduous, but when executed with forethought and vision, it provides bountiful rewards, both material and personal, an experience beyond comprehension. What you get from your Team will be directly related to what you give to it.

People often ask why I became a SEAL. My answer ... "for the Brotherhood!" *Never stop learning.* This will not nor should it be the last book about leadership!

CONCLUDING LESSON

- Challenge yourself to become a true leader.
- Build a solid foundation upon which to develop your team.
- Do not be risk averse.
- Study people and continually develop your leadership skills.
- If things are *too* smooth and no one is complaining, take a close look at operations and ensure that you are preventing complacency.
- Leadership is a priviledge; embrace all the trials, tribulations, and rewards that come with it.
- If it sucks, it will make a great story.
- ENJOY SUCCESS!